THE KIDS' FIFTY-STATE COOKBOOK

The Kids' Fifty-State Cookbook

• • •

by Aileen Paul

illustrated
by Earl Thollander

DOUBLEDAY & COMPANY, INC.

GARDEN CITY, NEW YORK

To my only brother, Don, with whom I shared the fun and difficulties of living in new places.

Library of Congress Cataloging in Publication Data

Paul, Aileen.
The kids' fifty-state cookbook.

Includes index.
SUMMARY: Cookbook for beginners containing easy recipes for the specialties of each state.
1. Cookery, American—Juvenile literature. [1. Cookery, American]
I. Thollander, Earl. II. Title. III. Title: Fifty-state cookbook.
TX715.P3238   641.5'973
ISBN: 0-385-11227-0 TRADE
0-385-11228-9 PREBOUND
LIBRARY OF CONGRESS CATALOG CARD NUMBER 76–2812

ACKNOWLEDGMENTS

My thanks to the adventuresome kids in my cooking classes; to family and friends; to helpful newspaper, radio, and television colleagues; to efficient state Chambers of Commerce; and to the dedicated Food and Nutrition Specialists, Extension Service, United States Department of Agriculture.

CONTENTS

INTRODUCTION

"Where do you get your recipes?" I'm often asked when teaching or visiting libraries and schools. The answer is that I create some, and many others come from family and friends. All, however, are tested in my Cooking School for Children.

For the recipes in this book—which come from every state—I talked to and wrote letters to people from all over the country. They were helpful and seemed to enjoy sharing their cooking suggestions.

And, as I was writing, bits of cooking information, long stored away in my memory, came to the surface. Because I have lived and traveled in every part of the United States, I have learned a lot about regional cooking, often without realizing it.

You see, I was born in Georgia. So were my father, and his mother and father. My mother, however, and her Swedish parents home-steaded in Kansas, Wyoming, and Nebraska, where I spent each summer of my childhood.

As a youngster, I lived in Georgia, Texas, New Mexico, and Colorado; as an adult, in Florida, Chicago, and New York City. Vacations and business trips have taken me to almost every state. Now, New Jersey is my home.

Writing this book has given me a chance to share many treasured American recipes with you. I hope that you will enjoy preparing them.

A WORD TO ADULTS

Those of you who know my books are aware that I think cooking is a rewarding and fun-filled experience for children.

When boys and girls cook with the recipes in this book—such as, Cow Belle Beefburgers from Wyoming or Black Walnut Cookies from Indiana—they acquire a vigorous appetite and some knowledge about the state the recipe came from. And they enjoy sharing the results of their cooking with family and friends.

I choose recipes for my cooking classes and books with the thought that seven- to ten-year-olds will probably be cooking with an adult conveniently near, and older children more on their own. So much, as you know, depends upon the child's cooking experience and manual ability, not age.

Children of all ages enjoy tidying up, too, when clean sponges, fresh towels, and pleasant-smelling soap are provided.

If you are concerned about children in the kitchen, I think you will be reassured by reading together the steps and rules in "About Cooking."

Grown-ups should stand by while the cooking goes on: to answer questions, help with the oven, pour hot liquids, whatever is needed by the young cook.

A WORD TO KIDS

You have a wide choice of things to cook in this book. Some foods are sweet, like Baked Fudge Custard from Oklahoma. Some are unusual, like Seneca Indian Stew from New York. Several might be useful on a camping trip, like Bannock from North Dakota. Others, like Dried Apples from Tennessee, could make an interesting class or club project.

Some of the recipes use foods that are grown or produced in the state, like Vermont's Maple Bars. Others originated with a group living in the state, like Pennsylvania Dutch Funnel Cakes. And still others are associated with a period in American history, like Pecan Waffles, a colonial recipe from Williamsburg, Virginia.

One thing you will notice about this book is the great variety of foods used. This is because we live in a vast country where many different kinds of foods are grown. We also have a rich heritage of cooking styles from settlers and immigrants from countries all over the world. I think you'll enjoy trying new things and learning about unusual foods eaten in other parts of the country. If some ingredients are hard to find in your area, I have suggested substitutes, or, in some cases, have given an address for a mail order.

Now let's think about the steps and rules to follow when you are cooking. To get the right results, you have to do the right thing at the right time.

ABOUT COOKING

There are definite *Steps* to be taken when cooking:

1. Read recipe carefully before you start.

2. Be sure you have all ingredients.

3. Place ingredients together.

4. Keep a garbage pail handy so you can clean up as you cook.

5. Put a damp sponge in a convenient spot to wipe up spills. And don't worry about a little mess.

Adults can be helpful. Depending upon your age, let an adult do the following:

1. Turn on, or light, the oven or the burners of the stove.

2. Help put in and remove foods from the oven.

3. Pour hot water, or drain hot foods.

Among the *Safety Rules,* be sure to:

1. Turn handles of pots and pans so they will not be knocked off stove or counter.

2. Use a *dry* pot holder, not a damp one, which carries heat.

3. Use a paring knife (the little one) for most of your cutting. Ask for help if you must use a different one.

4. Use a wooden chopping board for cutting. Most counter tops scratch easily.

5. Use electric mixer or blender only when an adult is there to supervise.

ABOUT THE RECIPES

To preheat means to light or turn on the oven to a certain temperature. Usually, it is step number one. However, you can save energy by preheating 10 minutes before use.

To blend is to mix several ingredients so that they look and feel like one ingredient.

To beat is to blend them hard enough to add air and make the mixture light.

To cover with water, the amount you use depends upon the size of the pan.

When measuring, be exact.

You can *substitute*
    Frozen, fresh, and canned foods for each other.
    Prepared dressings bought at the store for your own homemade ones.
    Butter, margarine, or shortening when greasing a pan.
    Onion powder or dehydrated onions for fresh ones.
    Prepared crumb pie shell from the store for your own.

Buy butter or margarine in sticks with tablespoons marked off.

Measurements for nuts are for shelled ones.

Fruits should be washed just before using. Wash berries a handful at a time.

When opening a can, you may need help because the edges are sharp. Wipe off top because dust sometimes settles there.

ABOUT UTENSILS

You probably know most of the utensils you will use in cooking, like measuring cups and egg beaters. But perhaps these pictures of other items may be helpful.

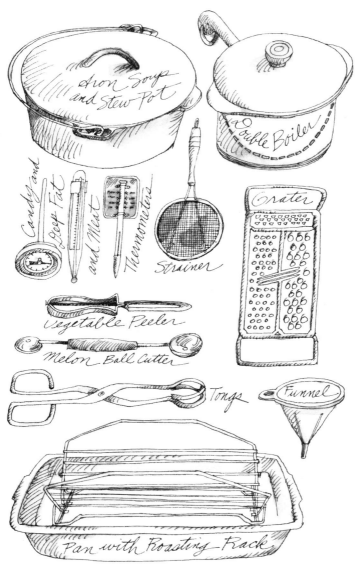

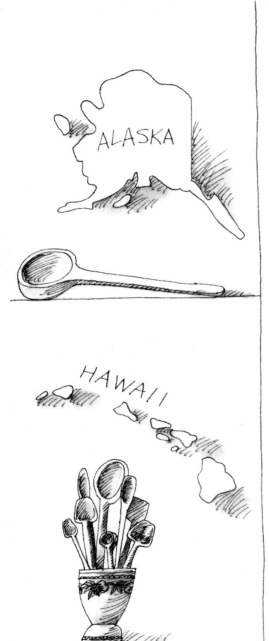
ALASKA

HAWAII

WASHINGTON
MONTANA
OREGON
IDAHO
CALIFORNIA
NEVADA
UTAH
ARIZONA

RECIPES FROM
THE FIFTY STATES

ALABAMA

The State Capitol at Montgomery

PEANUT COCONUT JEWELS

Alabama and its neighbor Georgia are the leading sources of peanuts in this country. Peanuts became important in the South when the cotton crop was ruined by the boll weevil. Farmers looked for other crops and Dr. George Washington Carver suggested peanuts.

Each year the National Peanut Festival is held at Dothan, Alabama, and features a recipe contest. This one was a favorite.

HERE'S WHAT YOU NEED:

1 cup peanut butter
½ cup honey
1 cup seedless raisins

1 teaspoon vanilla
1½ cups prepared flaked coconut

HERE'S WHAT YOU DO:

1. Measure and spoon peanut butter, honey, raisins, and vanilla into bowl. Mix thoroughly.

2. Measure coconut and spread on wax paper.

3. Drop spoonfuls of peanut mixture on coconut and roll lightly with finger tips to coat.

4. Place in refrigerator to chill.

MAKES ABOUT 36 SMALL CANDIES

QUICK GUMBO SOUP

Gumbo soups and stews are popular in Alabama. They show the influence of Creole cooking handed down by the original Spanish and French colonists, called Creoles, who lived there long ago.

Okra, a green vegetable grown and used mostly in the South, is one of the special ingredients of many Creole dishes. This is a quick version of old-fashioned gumbo soup.

HERE'S WHAT YOU NEED:

*1 can (11 ounces) beef broth
  (consommé)
¼ cup uncooked rice
1 cup okra (fresh,
  canned, or frozen)*

*1 can (1 pound) tomatoes
Salt and pepper
2 or 3 drops Tabasco sauce*

HERE'S WHAT YOU DO:

1. Open can of beef broth and pour into large pot. Add ½ can of water instead of 1 can as directed on label.

2. Place on medium heat and bring to a boil. Add rice and lower heat.

3. Add okra and tomatoes. (If okra is fresh, wash and cut into ½ inch pieces first.) Bring to boil again, lower heat, and cook for 30 minutes.

4. Salt and pepper to taste. Add 2 or 3 drops of Tabasco. (Measure carefully; it's a peppery liquid containing some of the spices that belong to Creole cooking.)

MAKES 4 TO 6 SERVINGS

FIG DESSERT

Figs grow well in southern Alabama, where the climate is mild. You can eat them fresh (peel the outer skin), or you can cook them. Figs are ripe when they are soft to the touch.

HERE'S WHAT YOU NEED:

½ cup brown sugar
1½ cups water

12 fresh ripe figs
⅓ cup pecans

HERE'S WHAT YOU DO:

1. Measure sugar and pour into medium-size saucepan.

2. Measure water and stir into sugar. Place over medium heat and bring to a boil to melt sugar. Remove from heat.

3. Peel figs with paring knife. (Do not try to remove stem.) Place figs in saucepan carefully to avoid splashing.

4. Return saucepan to medium or low heat and simmer for 5 to 8 minutes. Since figs are soft, do not overcook.

5. Cool figs and remove stems with paring knife.

6. Chop nuts on cutting board with paring knife.

7. Place 3 figs in each of four serving dishes with small amount of syrup left over from cooking. Sprinkle with chopped nuts.

MAKES 4 SERVINGS

Note: Canned figs or cooked dried figs can be substituted. No cooking would be required.

ALASKA

Sourdough prospector

SOURDOUGH PANCAKES

In Alaska and other western states, prospectors searching for gold in the 1800s were called "sourdoughs." The name came from the sourdough starter they carried on their wilderness trips.

The starter, used for making bread and pancakes, is a small amount of fermented batter or dough which is saved and stored each time.

The recipe is a project done in three steps, so you will want to plan ahead.

SOURDOUGH STARTER

HERE'S WHAT YOU NEED:

2⅓ cups lukewarm water   *1 tablespoon sugar*
1 envelope dry yeast powder   *2 cups flour*

HERE'S WHAT YOU DO:

1. Measure warm water into large glass mixing bowl. Sprinkle yeast over water. Stir to dissolve.

2. Measure and add sugar and flour. Beat until smooth.

3. Cover bowl with clean kitchen towel or double cheesecloth. Store in draft-free place (unheated oven) for 3 days. Stir twice a day.

4. Pour into glass jar. Set top loosely so that air can circulate and keep starter from spoiling.

MAKES 3½ CUPS STARTER.

Use as follows:

PANCAKE BATTER

HERE'S WHAT YOU NEED:

1 cup starter
2½ cups flour
2 cups water
1 egg
2 tablespoons vegetable oil or
  melted shortening

¼ cup cream or milk
1 teaspoon salt
1 teaspoon baking soda
2 tablespoons sugar

HERE'S WHAT YOU DO:

1. Begin preparation the night before (or 8 hours in advance). Measure and pour starter, flour, and water into large glass bowl.

2. Beat until smooth. Cover with clean kitchen towel or double cheesecloth. Place in draft-free area overnight.

3. The next morning, remove 1 cup of the mixture and add to starter in glass jar. Refrigerate to use again.

4. Break egg into bowl. Measure oil, cream, salt, baking soda, and sugar. Add to egg. Mix thoroughly, but do not overbeat.

5. Place lightly greased pancake griddle on medium to high heat. Pour small amounts of batter on griddle. Bake on one side until bubbles appear. Turn and brown lightly on other side.

MAKES ABOUT 16 PANCAKES, DEPENDING UPON SIZE

Note: Sourdough pancakes are light and must be turned carefully.

CANDIED ROSE HIPS

Fruit is expensive in Alaska since most of it must be shipped in by air. As a result, Alaskans are encouraged to use native berries and rose hips, the seed pods of garden and wild roses.

When picked after the first frost, rose hips are filled with health-giving vitamins. They have a nutlike flavor when dried or cooked. Use them in puddings, with fruit desserts, or in baked foods. These candied rose hips are a great snack.

HERE'S WHAT YOU NEED:

1 ½ cups rose hips
½ cup sugar
¼ cup water

HERE'S WHAT YOU DO:

1. Wash and remove the "tails" of rose hips. Cut rose hips in two and remove seeds with point of paring knife.

2. Measure sugar and water. Pour into medium-size saucepan. Bring to a boil.

3. Add rose hips and simmer over low heat for 10 minutes. Stir occasionally to keep from burning.

4. Drain through strainer. (You may need adult help.)

5. Place rose hips on cookie sheet and sprinkle lightly with sugar.

6. Place cookie sheet in sunny window for several days, or in slow oven (preheat to 200 degrees F.) for several hours.

7. Store between layers of wax paper in covered container to keep dry.

MAKES ABOUT 1 CUP

Note: Rose hips may be bought in health food stores and specialty shops.

ARIZONA

monument Valley

CHILI CON CARNE
(Chili Peppers with Meat)

Chili con carne is prepared in several different ways. This south-western recipe, which uses a solid cut of beef instead of the usual ground meat, is popular in Arizona. Chili peppers are referred to as "chilies" in Mexican cooking.

HERE'S WHAT YOU NEED:

1 ½ pounds beef, round or chuck
1 can (4 ounces) green chilies or 1 teaspoon chili powder

1 can (1 pound) tomatoes
1 teaspoon garlic powder
1 can (1 pound) kidney or frijole beans
1 teaspoon salt

HERE'S WHAT YOU DO:

1. Put beef in large pot and cover with water. Place on high heat and bring to a boil. Lower heat, cover, and simmer for about 1 hour.

2. Chop drained chilies and tomatoes with paring knife. Add to beef along with garlic powder. Simmer 1 ½ hours, or until meat is tender when pierced with a fork.

3. Remove meat to plate. Cut into small pieces. Return to pot (You may need help.)

4. Add drained beans and continue cooking until they are heated. Season with salt, if needed.

MAKES 4 SERVINGS

Note: Green chilies are canned and distributed to stores by the El Paso Co., El Paso, Texas 88021. You can write for the name and address of a store near you that carries them.

GRAPEFRUIT AND MELON SALAD

Grapefruits are grown on the irrigated lands of Arizona. The moist, tart fruit will quench your thirst on dry desert days. It is delicious alone or with other fruits.

HERE'S WHAT YOU NEED:

2 grapefruits
1 cantaloupe or honeydew melon

Lettuce
Honey Salad Dressing (see page 121)

HERE'S WHAT YOU DO:

1. Peel grapefruits and melon. Cut in thin slices. (You may need help with cutting.)

2. Place lettuce leaves on platter. Arrange slices of grapefruit and melon alternately.

3. Prepare dressing and sprinkle over salad.

MAKES 4 TO 6 SERVINGS

ARKANSAS

Farm country

OZARK PUDDING

The Ozark Mountains run through Arkansas, Missouri, and Oklahoma. This recipe is said to have been a favorite of the late President Harry S Truman.

HERE'S WHAT YOU NEED:

*Small amount of shortening
   to grease pan
2 eggs
¾ cup sugar
2 tablespoons flour*

*⅛ teaspoon salt
½ teaspoon baking powder
½ cup walnuts or pecans
1 medium-size tart apple*

HERE'S WHAT YOU DO:

1. Preheat oven to 325 degrees F. Grease 8-inch pie pan.

2. Break eggs into bowl and beat lightly.

3. Measure sugar and pour slowly into eggs, mixing as you pour.

4. Measure flour, salt, and baking powder. Blend together. Add to eggs, stirring until smooth.

5. Chop nuts on wooden cutting board with paring knife.

6. Peel apple. Core, and chop enough for ½ cup.

7. Add nuts and apples to bowl. Mix well.

8. Pour mixture into pie pan and bake for 30 minutes.

Serve with ice cream or cream.

MAKES 4 SERVINGS

WATERMELON BOAT

This watermelon boat is fun to serve on special occasions.

HERE'S WHAT YOU NEED:

1 small watermelon
2 pounds white seedless grapes

HERE'S WHAT YOU DO:

1. Cut watermelon lengthwise in half. Remove one half, cover and refrigerate for later use. (You may need adult help.)

2. Cut around the remaining melon half close to the rind, leaving a thin rim of red beyond the white.

3. Take the fruit out of the melon and remove the seeds. Form balls of the fruit with melon ball cutter or cut into cubes.

4. Cut grapes in half, saving one small cluster for decoration. Mix grapes and melon.

5. Return fruit to melon shell. Place cluster of grapes at center.

MAKES 10 SERVINGS

15

CALIFORNIA

Cable car, San Francisco

ORANGE SHERBET

Among the flavorful citrus fruits grown in California are oranges. You can eat them sliced, in salads, or in a sherbet like this one. Homemade sherbets take time to prepare, but they are well worth it.

HERE'S WHAT YOU NEED:

3 or 4 oranges
1 cup sugar

¾ cup corn syrup
2 cups water

HERE'S WHAT YOU DO:

1. Grate orange rind, enough for 1 tablespoon.

2. Measure and pour sugar, corn syrup, orange rind, and 2 cups of water into saucepan. Place over low heat and stir until sugar is melted.

3. Remove from heat and cool syrup.

4. Squeeze 2 cups of orange juice and add to cooled syrup.

5. Pour into refrigerator ice trays. Place in freezer and freeze until firm.

6. Place mixing bowl and beaters in refrigerator to chill.

7. Remove frozen mixture from tray to bowl and break up with spoon. Beat with electric mixer or egg beater until it becomes a thick mush.

8. Spoon back into trays. Return to refrigerator and freeze again.

MAKES 4 SERVINGS

EASY RECIPE

MIXED GREEN SALAD

In California's open markets and supermarkets there are many kinds of salad greens sold. The different flavors, textures, and colors make an interesting salad without adding other vegetables.

HERE'S WHAT YOU NEED:

2 cups soft-leaved lettuce, like Bibb or Boston
2 cups stiff-leaved lettuce, like Cos or romaine

2 cups crisp lettuce, like iceberg
Salad Dressing (see page 183)

HERE'S WHAT YOU DO:

1. Place salad bowl in refrigerator to cool.

2. Wash lettuce and drain well. Place in refrigerator to make it crisp. If not using immediately, cover with transparent wrap or place in vegetable compartment of refrigerator.

3. Prepare salad dressing.

4. Tear salad greens into pieces and place in chilled salad bowl. Sprinkle salad dressing and toss greens gently. Take care to pour only as much dressing as needed to coat leaves.

MAKES 4 TO 6 SERVINGS

EGG FOO YUNG

San Francisco is a beautiful city perched on hills between the Pacific Ocean and the busy bay. Its Chinatown is an attraction for tourists and residents alike. Many Chinese recipes are complicated to prepare, but I think you will find this one quite easy.

HERE'S WHAT YOU NEED:

1 thin slice boiled ham
1 tablespoon drained fresh or
*   canned bean sprouts*
½ teaspoon onion salt

½ teaspoon soy sauce
2 eggs
Small amount of oil

HERE'S WHAT YOU DO:

1. Chop ham, enough for 1 tablespoon.

2. Measure and mix together ham, bean sprouts, onion salt, and soy sauce.

3. Break eggs into bowl and beat lightly.

4. Cover bottom of small fry pan with oil, unless pan is Teflon-coated. Place over medium to low heat.

5. Combine and mix ingredients. Pour into pan and fry until cooked on one side. Turn and fry on the other side.

MAKES 1 OR 2 SERVINGS

Note: Serve with additional soy sauce.

COLORADO

Cliff palace, Mesa Verde National Park

CANTALOUPE SALAD

Rocky Ford cantaloupes and honeydew melons are raised near the Arkansas River in the southeast part of Colorado.

HERE'S WHAT YOU NEED:

2 small cantaloupes
1 pint cottage cheese
Lettuce

HERE'S WHAT YOU DO:

1. Slice cantaloupes in half and remove seeds with spoon.

2. Fill halves of fruit with cottage cheese.

3. Place on lettuce leaves on individual salad plates.

MAKES 4 SERVINGS

PIKES PEAK COOLER

I guess you drink this beverage when you get to the top of the mountain.

HERE'S WHAT YOU NEED:

1 egg
1 lemon
3 to 4 tablespoons sugar

1 cup cider
Sprinkle of nutmeg

(CONTINUED ON NEXT PAGE)

HERE'S WHAT YOU DO:

1. Break egg into bowl and beat until frothy.

2. Squeeze juice from lemon, and pour gradually into egg, stirring constantly.

3. Measure and add sugar, and stir until dissolved. The less sugar you use, the better for you.

4. Measure and add cider. Mix and sprinkle with nutmeg.

MAKES 2 SERVINGS

DENVER SANDWICHES

One story says that Denver sandwiches were created by a cook for the railroad crews putting down the first rails into Denver in 1870. The men got tired of fried egg sandwiches and threatened to run the cook out of town if he didn't come up with something different. And he did.

HERE'S WHAT YOU NEED:

¼ pound sliced bacon
Butter, softened
8 slices bread
1 small onion

1 small green pepper
3 eggs
Salt and pepper

HERE'S WHAT YOU DO:

1. Fry bacon until crisp in fry pan over medium heat.

2. While bacon is frying, butter bread. Chop onion and green pepper on cutting board with paring knife.

22

3. Remove bacon from pan and drain on brown paper or paper towels.

4. Cook onions and green pepper in hot bacon grease several minutes until softened, but not brown.

5. Take fry pan off heat and remove extra bacon grease with large kitchen spoon, leaving about 1 tablespoon grease along with onions and pepper. Return fry pan to heat.

6. Break eggs into bowl and beat with egg beater. Pour into fry pan. Add crumbled bacon. Sprinkle with salt and pepper. Stir gently as eggs cook until golden brown on one side. Turn with wide spatula and cook on other side.

7. Cut into four wedges and serve between slices of buttered bread.

MAKES 4 SANDWICHES

CONNECTICUT

Church on the Common

QUICK BROWN BREAD

From colonial times until today, boys and girls have enjoyed hot breads. This recipe was originally steamed in a kettle over low flames in the fireplace. You will, of course, use the modern oven in your kitchen, but you can keep this recipe in mind for campfire cooking.

HERE'S WHAT YOU NEED:

Small amount of shortening to grease pan
2 cups whole wheat flour
1 teaspoon salt
½ teaspoon baking soda

1½ teaspoons baking powder
1 egg
1 cup buttermilk or sour milk
½ cup molasses
¼ cup vegetable oil

HERE'S WHAT YOU DO:

1. Preheat oven to 350 degrees F. Grease 7×11-inch pan.

2. Measure and mix flour, salt, soda, and baking powder thoroughly.

3. Break egg into large bowl and beat with egg beater.

4. Measure and add buttermilk, molasses, and vegetable oil to egg.

5. Add liquid ingredients to flour mixture. Stir only enough to mix.

6. Pour into pan and bake for about 30 minutes. Remember to use pot holders.

MAKES 10 TO 12 SLICES

25

PUMPKIN PIE

The first "pumpkin pie" was probably made by slicing off the pumpkin top, removing the seeds, and filling it with milk and spices. A natural sweetener, such as honey, was added and the pumpkin baked in the ashes. It might be fun to try sometime, but you'll have better results with the following recipe.

HERE'S WHAT YOU NEED:

2 eggs
½ cup brown sugar
2 tablespoons molasses
1 teaspoon salt
1 teaspoon cinnamon
½ teaspoon nutmeg

½ teaspoon ginger
1½ cups milk
1½ cups canned pumpkin
1 9-inch unbaked cereal pie
    shell (*see page 182*)

HERE'S WHAT YOU DO:

1. Preheat oven to 450 degrees F.

2. Break eggs into large bowl. Beat lightly.

3. Measure and add brown sugar, molasses, salt, and spices. Mix thoroughly.

4. Gradually stir in milk.

5. Add pumpkin to mixture and blend.

6. Pour into pie shell. Bake for 10 minutes at 450 degrees F. Lower heat to 325 degrees F. and bake 30 or 40 minutes or until table knife inserted in center comes out clean. Use pot holders.

MAKES 6 SERVINGS

DELAWARE

Daybreak Castle

PEACH MELBA

In the spring, Delaware is fragrant with blossoms from the peach trees grown throughout the state.

HERE'S WHAT YOU NEED:

1 cup fresh or frozen raspberries
2 ripe peaches
1 pint vanilla ice cream

HERE'S WHAT YOU DO:

1. Wash raspberries, if fresh, and drain through strainer. If frozen, open package of raspberries and let thaw while getting peaches ready.

2. Wash peaches and peel. Slice in half and remove pits.

3. Pour raspberries into blender and blend on high to count of three to make a sauce, or mash with fork.

4. Put a serving of ice cream in the bottom of four pretty glass dishes. Top each with peach half and raspberries.

MAKES 4 SERVINGS

DELMARVA CHEESY CHICKEN

The Delmarva Chicken Festival, held each year since 1947, has been the source of many "lickin' good" chicken recipes from Delaware, Maryland, and Virginia. Families come to have fun and to sample fried chicken cooked in a ten-foot fry pan—the largest one in the world. The following recipe was a winner.

28

HERE'S WHAT YOU NEED:

1 cup cornflake crumbs
¼ cup grated Parmesan
  cheese
2 tablespoons parsley flakes
1 teaspoon salt
½ teaspoon paprika (may be omitted)

⅛ teaspoon pepper
½ cup butter or margarine
1 broiler-fryer chicken (2½ to 3 pounds), cut up

HERE'S WHAT YOU DO:

1. Lightly grease baking sheet or shallow baking dish.

2. Measure all of the ingredients, except the butter and chicken, and mix in a heavy brown paper or clean plastic bag.

3. Melt butter in saucepan. Remove from heat.

4. Preheat oven to 375 degrees F.

5. Dip chicken in melted butter with fork or tongs. Drop 2 or 3 pieces of chicken at a time into crumb mixture. Shake bag to coat chicken.

6. Place chicken on baking sheet or in baking dish.

7. Bake 1 hour or until brown and tender when pierced with fork.

MAKES 4 TO 5 SERVINGS

Note: Cornflake crumbs and grated Parmesan cheese may be bought at most supermarkets.

FLORIDA

The beach at Miami

JELLIED TANGERINES

Much of the farm land of Florida is covered with groves of citrus fruits. Oranges, grapefruits, lemons, and tangerines make up more than one third of Florida's total farm income.

Tangerines have a delicate but spicy and tart flavor. They can be eaten raw, in salads, and in desserts.

HERE'S WHAT YOU NEED:

1 3-ounce package orange-flavored gelatin
2 small tangerines
8 ice cubes

HERE'S WHAT YOU DO:

1. Boil water in teakettle.

2. While water is coming to a boil, peel tangerines and separate sections. Remove stringy white fiber and seeds.

3. Empty package of gelatin into mixing bowl. Measure 1 cup of boiling water. (You may need adult help.) Add to gelatin and mix until powder is dissolved.

4. Add ice cubes and continue stirring until mixture thickens, about 3 minutes. Remove any unmelted ice.

5. Stir tangerine sections into thickened gelatin.

6. Pour into small serving dishes and chill in refrigerator until firm, about 20 minutes.

MAKES 4 SERVINGS

Note: Lemon-flavored gelatin may be substituted.

31

KEY LIME PIE

Limes are small, green citrus fruits that grow only in hot climates. There are two kinds of limes: a larger variety known as the Persian lime, and a smaller kind called the Key lime, which grows in the Florida Keys, small islands off the southern tip of Florida. You can use either fruit in this no-bake recipe.

HERE'S WHAT YOU NEED:

1 8-inch crumb pie shell (see page 181)
3 eggs
1 can (14 ounces) condensed *milk*

3 to 5 limes, enough for ½ cup juice

HERE'S WHAT YOU DO:

1. Prepare crumb pie shell.

2. Separate egg yolks from whites (see page 179).

3. Beat egg yolks until creamy but do not overbeat.

4. Add condensed milk slowly to egg yolks, continuing to beat. (A rubber scraper is helpful in removing milk from can.)

5. Squeeze limes.

6. Add lime juice, small amount at a time, continuing to beat.

7. Wash beater and dry. Beat egg whites until they are stiff and peaks form when you lift beater.

8. Slowly stir beaten whites, one third at a time, into the yolk, milk, and juice mixture. Blend gently so that no bits of white can be seen.

9. Spoon into pie shell. Cover lightly with transparent plastic wrap and place in refrigerator. Chill at least 4 hours or longer.

MAKES 6 TO 8 SERVINGS

Note: Bottled lime juice may be used, but fresh is preferred. Place any leftover pie in refrigerator so that it will not spoil.

GEORGIA

Stone Mountain near Atlanta

TURNIP GREENS

Turnip greens cooked in the following manner have long been popular in the South. The liquid in which they are cooked is sometimes called "pot likker." According to a Georgia tradition, if turnip greens are served on New Year's Day, those present at the meal will have money to spare throughout the coming year.

HERE'S WHAT YOU NEED:

½ pound salt pork or bacon	*2 pounds turnip greens*
1 quart water	*Salt and pepper*

HERE'S WHAT YOU DO:

1. Place salt pork in large saucepan. Cover with water, about 1 quart. Place over high heat and bring to a boil. Lower heat and simmer for ½ hour.

2. While salt pork is cooking, wash turnip greens (see page 179).

3. Place greens in a saucepan with salt pork. Bring to a boil again and then lower to medium heat. Cook until tender, about 30 minutes.

4. Remove salt pork and slice.

5. Drain greens through strainer into another saucepan. (Ask an adult for help if you need it.) Place saucepan over low heat to keep "pot likker" hot.

6. Chop greens fine and season with salt and pepper. Place in deep serving bowl. Pour about 1 cup of hot liquid over greens and arrange salt pork slices on top.

MAKES 4 TO 6 SERVINGS

Note: If you want to use frozen turnip greens, begin as directed with salt pork and add greens after ½ hour. Cook according to time on package.

35

EASY AMBROSIA

Ambrosia, a dessert of oranges and coconut, is usually served at Christmas or New Year's dinner along with fruit cake.

HERE'S WHAT YOU NEED:

> *2 cans (11 ounces) mandarin orange segments*
> *½ to ¾ cup packaged grated coconut*

HERE'S WHAT YOU DO:

1. Open and drain orange sections, leaving some liquid. Place in bowl.

2. Gently stir coconut into oranges. Cover and place in refrigerator to chill.

3. Serve in sherbet dishes.

MAKES 4 TO 6 SERVINGS

Note: You may use fresh oranges instead of canned, if you wish.

BOILED GREEN PEANUTS

Many boys and girls in small towns or the country learn how to boil uncooked peanuts, a favorite snack with a salty taste. Raw peanuts can usually be bought at grocery stores or roadside stands in Georgia.

HERE'S WHAT YOU NEED:

3 quarts green (uncooked) peanuts
2 quarts water
½ cup salt

HERE'S WHAT YOU DO:

1. Wash green unshelled peanuts thoroughly under running water. Remove stems.

2. Mix approximately 2 quarts water and salt in large saucepan. Place peanuts in water (there should be enough to cover). Boil 35 to 40 minutes until tender. Taste to see if they are tender; the texture should be similar to that of a cooked bean. Add more salt if needed.

3. Remove the peanuts with a slotted spoon or ask a grown-up to pour off the hot water. Shell and eat, hot or cold.

MAKES ABOUT 4½ CUPS SHELLED PEANUTS

HAWAII

The Surfer

PORK CHOPS WAIKIKI

Pork is a favorite meat in the islands.

HERE'S WHAT YOU NEED:

*Small amount of shortening
  to grease casserole
1 large or 2 small oranges
4 medium-size pork chops*

*1 tablespoon flour
4 slices canned pineapple
  with juice
About ¼ cup of water*

HERE'S WHAT YOU DO:

1. Preheat oven to 350 degrees F. Grease shallow casserole.

2. Peel and cut orange in quarters.

3. Sprinkle pork chops lightly with flour on both sides.

4. Arrange meat in casserole with orange quarters in between chops. Add small amount of water to cover bottom of pan. Cover and bake for about 20 minutes.

5. Remove from oven using pot holders. (You may need adult help.) Turn pork chops and place pineapple slices on each. Add juice if casserole is dry.

6. Return to oven and bake for another 40 minutes.

MAKES 4 SERVINGS

HAWAIIAN PUNCH BOWL

Hawaiian celebration feasts are called luaus. Food may be simple or elaborate. The luau is not complete, however, without a punch bowl of frosty, refreshing fruit juices.

HERE'S WHAT YOU NEED:

*1 can (46 ounces) pineapple
    juice
1 can (6 ounces) frozen
    orange juice
1 can (6 ounces) frozen
    lemonade*

*1 quart cherry soda
1 quart club soda
2 trays ice cubes*

HERE'S WHAT YOU DO:

1. Pour pineapple juice into punch bowl.

2. Prepare frozen lemonade and orange juice as directed on can using half the amount of water called for. Pour into bowl.

3. Add cherry soda, club soda, and ice. Stir and serve chilled.

MAKES ABOUT 16 LARGE OR 32 SMALL SERVINGS

IDAHO

Rider near War Eagle mountain

BAKED POTATOES

Idaho is famous for its potatoes, which are especially suited for baking. They are grown on the rich plains.

HERE'S WHAT YOU NEED:

4 medium-size baking potatoes
Butter or vegetable shortening
Salt and pepper

HERE'S WHAT YOU DO:

1. Preheat oven to 425 degrees F.

2. Wash potatoes under running water, scrubbing with vegetable brush. The skins should be clean because they are good to eat. Dry with towel.

3. Rub butter or shortening over each potato.

4. Place potatoes directly on oven rack, not too close together.

5. Bake until done, about 45 minutes. At that time remove 1 potato from oven (use pot holders) and squeeze potato gently with towel. If soft, potatoes are done. If still hard, return to oven for another 10 or 15 minutes to finish baking.

6. When potatoes are cooked, remove from oven with pot holders.

7. Cut slits crosswise on top of each using paring knife. Place a pat of butter on opened potato. Sprinkle with salt and pepper to taste.

ALLOW 1 POTATO PER PERSON

LENTIL LOAF

The states of Idaho and Washington produce the entire lentil crop of the United States. This meatless dish is an appetizing substitute for meat loaf.

HERE'S WHAT YOU NEED:

Small amount of shortening
  to grease pan
½ cup walnuts
1 egg
1 small can (5⅓ ounces)
  evaporated milk

2 cups cooked lentils
½ teaspoon sage
1 teaspoon onion salt
2 tablespoons vegetable oil
1 cup bread crumbs

HERE'S WHAT YOU DO:

1. Preheat oven to 350 degrees F. Grease 9×5-inch loaf pan.

2. Chop nuts on wooden cutting board with paring knife.

3. Break egg into cup or small bowl and beat lightly with fork. Add milk.

4. Measure lentils, sage, onion salt, oil, and bread crumbs into large bowl. Add egg mixture and nuts. Mix well.

5. Spoon into loaf pan and bake 1 hour. Remember to use pot holders.

MAKES 6 TO 8 SERVINGS

Note: You might ask an adult to prepare lentils for another recipe and put aside 2 cups for you.

ILLINOIS

The home of Abraham Lincoln, Springfield

BAKED RICE PUDDING

Rice pudding is popular among Scandinavians. It may be cooked on top of the stove or baked. You may use raw or cooked rice. This recipe uses cooked rice.

HERE'S WHAT YOU NEED:

4 eggs
1 cup sugar
½ teaspoon salt
1 teaspoon cinnamon

1 quart milk
2 cups cooked rice
2 tablespoons butter,
  approximately

HERE'S WHAT YOU DO:

1. Preheat oven to 250 degrees F. Butter 9×13-inch baking dish.

2. Break eggs into bowl and beat lightly with beater or fork.

3. Measure and add sugar, salt, and cinnamon. Beat again.

4. Add milk and rice. Mix together.

5. Pour slowly into baking dish. Dot with butter.

6. Place in oven and bake about 1½ hours. (Use pot holders.)

MAKES 8 SERVINGS

KIELBASA SAUSAGE
(Kolbasi or Kolbassy)

In the 1800s Illinois drew many immigrants from Italy, Ireland, Germany, Poland, and the Scandinavian countries. Many continued to eat foods from their native countries, like this highly spiced Polish sausage, kielbasa.

HERE'S WHAT YOU NEED:

3 pounds kielbasa sausage

HERE'S WHAT YOU DO:

1. Place sausage links in deep fry pan. Cover with water. Place over medium to high heat and bring to a boil.

2. Lower heat and simmer for 30 minutes.

3. Remove with tongs or fork. Cut into slices. May be served hot or cold.

MAKES 4 SERVINGS

Note: Other spicy sausage may be substituted.

GERMAN SCRAMBLED EGGS

Many Germans settled in the large cities of Illinois. This recipe was a specialty of a German restaurant on the Near North Side of Chicago, where it was always served with crisp, pan-fried potatoes.

HERE'S WHAT YOU NEED:

6 eggs
¼ cup cream or milk
2 to 4 tablespoons butter

2 cooked frankfurters
2 teaspoons onion salt
⅛ teaspoon pepper

HERE'S WHAT YOU DO:

1. Break eggs into medium-size bowl. Add cream and beat lightly.

2. Melt butter in fry pan over low heat, enough to cover bottom.

3. While butter is melting, cut frankfurters in thin circles.

4. Pour eggs into skillet. Cook until they begin to thicken. Sprinkle with onion salt and pepper and add frankfurter circles.

5. Continue to cook, stirring gently until soft and fluffy.

MAKES 6 SERVINGS

INDIANA

Farmer in the corn

PERSIMMON PUDDING

An annual Persimmon Festival has been held in Mitchell, Indiana, since 1946. Sometimes the festival begins at the reconstructed Spring Mill Village in the state park.

Persimmons are native to Indiana and still grow wild. However, the fruit is grown commercially in southern states and California, and is available in the markets during the winter.

The smooth-skinned orange fruit must be ripe to be eaten, soft to the touch, but still firm.

HERE'S WHAT YOU NEED:

1 tablespoon butter or
 margarine
1 cup flour
½ teaspoon salt
½ teaspoon baking soda
¾ cup brown sugar

2 eggs
1 cup milk
1 tablespoon vegetable oil
1 or 2 ripe persimmons,
 enough to make 1 cup pulp

HERE'S WHAT YOU DO:

1. Preheat oven to 350 degrees F. Grease 8×8-inch baking pan generously with butter or margarine.

2. Measure flour, salt, baking soda, and sugar together.

3. Break eggs into large mixing bowl. Measure and add milk and oil. Beat lightly.

4. Peel persimmon and cut into small pieces. Place in blender and blend until smooth (with adult help), or mash with fork. Add to liquids.

5. Stir dry ingredients into liquids. Mix well.

(CONTINUED ON NEXT PAGE)

6. Pour batter into baking dish.

7. Bake for 50 minutes. (Remember to use pot holders.)

Serve warm with cream.

MAKES 4 SERVINGS

BLACK WALNUT COOKIES

If you live in Indiana, perhaps there are black walnut trees growing in your yard or nearby. Their unique flavor is valued today as it was in pioneer times. The same amount of work is still needed, however, to shuck off the outer shell and try to wash away the walnut stain from your hands.

HERE'S WHAT YOU NEED:

*Small amount of shortening
    to grease baking sheet
½ cup black walnuts
1 cup flour
¼ teaspoon baking powder*

*½ teaspoon salt
¼ teaspoon cinnamon
1 egg
1 cup brown sugar
1 teaspoon vanilla*

HERE'S WHAT YOU DO:

1. Preheat oven to 350 degrees F.

2. Grease baking sheet.

3. Chop nuts on cutting board using paring knife.

4. Measure 1 cup flour. Measure baking powder, salt, and cinnamon and stir into flour gently.

50

5. Beat egg in medium-size bowl until fluffy. Measure and add sugar gradually, continuing to beat. Measure and stir in vanilla.

6. Add dry ingredients and mix well. Stir in chopped nuts.

7. Drop by teaspoonfuls 3 inches apart on greased cookie sheet. Flatten with back of fork. Bake 10 to 12 minutes. Be sure to use pot holders.

MAKES 3 DOZEN COOKIES

Note: If canned black walnuts are not available at your supermarket or specialty shop, substitute English walnuts, generally referred to as California.

IOWA

The hog-farmer

CORN ON THE COB

Corn in Iowa is raised for eating, for popping, and for feeding to animals.

HERE'S WHAT YOU NEED:

1 tablespoon salt
1½ teaspoons sugar
8 ears fresh corn

HERE'S WHAT YOU DO:

1. Fill large kettle two thirds full of water. There must be enough to cover the corn, but not spill over. Measure and add salt and sugar. Place kettle on high heat.

2. While water is coming to a rolling boil, remove husks and silk from ears of corn, stripping from top to bottom.

3. Place 4 ears of corn in boiling water very carefully. Cook 4 to 6 minutes. Do not attempt to boil more than 4 ears at a time. Remove with tongs at end of cooking period, and cook remaining 4 ears.

Serve with butter.

ALLOW 2 EARS OF CORN PER PERSON

AMANA COOKIES

Among the early settlers in Iowa was a German religious group called the Ebenezer Society. They built the village of Amana along the Iowa River in 1855, and six more villages later.

Today the Amana Society welcomes visitors to their unusual community, where these cookies are available in their shops and restaurants.

HERE'S WHAT YOU NEED:

*Small amount of shortening
   to grease baking sheet*
2 eggs
2 cups brown sugar

2 to 2½ cups flour
½ teaspoon baking soda
½ teaspoon cinnamon

HERE'S WHAT YOU DO:

1. Break eggs into large bowl.

2. Measure sugar and add to eggs, stirring until completely blended.

3. Measure 2 cups of flour (put remaining flour aside to be used if needed), soda, and cinnamon together. Stir.

4. Add dry ingredients to egg-sugar mixture, and beat until thoroughly mixed. Dough should be soft but not too sticky to handle. If necessary, stir in additional flour.

5. Sprinkle flour lightly on a piece of transparent plastic wrap and spoon dough on it. Chill in refrigerator several hours, or freezer about 15 minutes.

6. Preheat oven to 325 degrees F. Grease baking sheets.

7. Roll out dough on lightly floured board to ⅛-inch thickness. Cut with floured round cookie cutter. Place on baking sheets.

8. Bake 20 minutes. (Use pot holders.)

MAKES ABOUT 60 COOKIES

KANSAS

Threshing grain

SWEDISH RUSK
(Sweetened Crusty Bread)

In 1868, a colony of Swedish immigrants pioneered co-operative farming in Smoky Valley, Kansas. Every other year the 3-day festival called *Svensk Hyllningsfest* takes place in Lindsborg in honor of those pioneers. There are Swedish dances, folk songs, arts and crafts, and unforgettable food.

There are several recipes for rusk, a Scandinavian favorite, and one of them is always on the *smörgåsbord* (the Swedish buffet table).

This is a recipe for older boys and girls.

HERE'S WHAT YOU NEED:

*Small amount of shortening
  to grease pan
1 stick (½ cup) butter
2 cups sugar
1 egg
5 cups flour*

*1 teaspoon baking powder
½ teaspoon salt
1 cup sour cream or
  buttermilk
1 cup pecans or walnuts*

HERE'S WHAT YOU DO:

1. Preheat oven to 350 degrees F. Grease 9×13-inch pan lightly.

2. Place butter in large bowl. Soften by beating with wooden spoon or mixer. Measure and gradually add sugar, stirring after each half cup.

3. Add egg and beat until blended.

4. Measure flour, baking powder, and salt. Mix together.

5. Measure sour cream. Add dry ingredients alternately with sour cream to butter-sugar mixture, beating after each time. (Alternately means to add first one and then the other.)

(CONTINUED ON NEXT PAGE)

6. Chop nuts on cutting board with paring knife and add to dough.

7. Spoon dough on pan and spread smooth with kitchen knife or narrow metal spatula. Bake about 30 minutes.

8. Remove from oven using pot holders and lower temperature to 300 degrees F. Cut in strips about ½ inch wide and 3 inches long. Return to oven for another 30 minutes, or until light brown.

MAKES 60 TO 70 PIECES

ROAST TENDERLOIN OF BEEF

Recently the President of the United States ate dinner in the home of the governor of Kansas. The main course, appropriately enough, was a roast tenderloin of beef, since Kansas is one of our great beef-producing states.

The preparation of a roast is very simple. It is the quality of the meat and the timing that make the beef tender and delicious. You may need help from an adult with the oven and carving later.

HERE'S WHAT YOU NEED:

1 tenderloin of beef (3 pounds)

HERE'S WHAT YOU DO:

1. Preheat oven to 325 degrees F.

2. Place beef on rack in shallow open roasting pan. Do not add water.

3. Place pan in oven and roast beef 35 minutes per pound for medium-rare, 42 minutes per pound for well done. A meat thermometer is useful if you have one.

4. Salt and pepper as desired after meat is cooked.

MAKES 6 SERVINGS

59

KENTUCKY

Blue Grass Country

KENTUCKY FRIED CHICKEN

Because Kentucky fried chicken calls for frying in a considerable amount of fat, this recipe is for you older, more experienced cooks. If you remove the fry pan from the heat when you add and turn the chicken pieces there is less chance of spattering.

HERE'S WHAT YOU NEED:

1 frying chicken (2 pounds),   *¾ teaspoon salt*
  cut in pieces   *⅛ teaspoon pepper*
½ cup flour   *½ cup (1 stick) butter*

HERE'S WHAT YOU DO:

1. Wash chicken and pat dry with paper towels.

2. Measure and pour flour, salt, and pepper into sturdy brown paper bag.

3. Place deep fry pan on medium to high heat. Melt butter in pan.

4. Place a few pieces of chicken at a time into bag and shake two or three times.

5. Carefully place flour-coated chicken in hot butter, and brown quickly on each side.

6. Lower heat, cover, and fry until tender, about 40 minutes.

7. Remove cover, turn pieces, and cook 10 minutes more for crispness.

8. Lift chicken from fry pan, drain on brown paper.

MAKES 4 TO 5 SERVINGS

ICED MINT TEA

Tea should not be an everyday drink, but for special occasions, you might enjoy this recipe. The mint and orange give a delicious flavor.

HERE'S WHAT YOU NEED:

1 cup sugar, or less
½ cup water
3 medium-size oranges
8 or 9 sprigs mint or 1
tablespoon dried mint

6 cups strong unsugared
instant tea or regular tea
(see page 184)
2 trays ice cubes

HERE'S WHAT YOU DO:

1. Measure sugar and water and pour into saucepan.

2. Grate rind from 1 orange. Add to sugar and water. Place saucepan over medium heat and boil for 5 minutes. Remove from heat and add crushed leaves of mint or dried mint.

3. Squeeze oranges and stir juice into liquid. Cool.

4. Measure and pour tea into pitcher.

5. Sweeten tea to taste with cooled mint syrup.

6. Fill tall glasses with ice and add tea.

MAKES 12 TO 14 SERVINGS

LOUISIANA

Bound for New Orleans

JAMBALAYA

The Spanish and French colonists in Louisiana, who were called Creoles, have kept their unique language and culture for several centuries. Their influence, including their style of cooking, is still felt today.

Creole seasoning is produced by combinations of red pepper, onions, garlic, okra, green peppers, and spices. Jambalaya is a Creole stew. This particular recipe uses ham and sausage, but different meats, poultry, and fish can be used.

HERE'S WHAT YOU NEED:

2 tablespoons butter	½ teaspoon garlic powder
6 small pork sausages	½ teaspoon thyme
1 small onion	1 teaspoon salt
1 small red pepper	⅛ teaspoon pepper
4 sprigs parsley or 1 teaspoon dried parsley	2 cups water
1 tablespoon flour	⅓ cup uncooked rice
1 can (6 ounces) tomato paste	½ pound cooked ham, cut up

HERE'S WHAT YOU DO:

1. Melt small amount of butter in large fry pan, enough to cover bottom, over medium heat.

2. Slice sausages, and cook slowly until brown. Turn as needed.

3. Chop onion, red pepper, and parsley while sausage is frying.

4. Add remaining butter to fry pan, if pan is dry, and spoon in onions and red pepper. Fry until soft.

5. Measure and stir in flour. Cook several minutes. Add tomato paste and mix until smooth with flour blended in.

64

6. Measure and add garlic powder, chopped parsley, thyme, salt, pepper, and 2 cups water. Bring to a boil. Lower heat and simmer for 5 minutes.

7. Measure and add rice and ham. Cover and cook until rice is tender and has absorbed liquid, about 20 minutes.

MAKES 4 SERVINGS

BAKED BANANAS

In New Orleans, this dish is also prepared with plantains, a tropical fruit similar to bananas.

HERE'S WHAT YOU NEED:

4 bananas that are not
  overripe
½ cup (1 stick) butter
½ cup light brown sugar

2 teaspoons artificial rum
  flavoring
2 tablespoons orange juice

HERE'S WHAT YOU DO:

1. Preheat oven to 400 degrees F. Butter shallow baking dish.

2. Peel and slice bananas in quarters. Place split side up in dish.

3. Dot with butter; sprinkle with sugar, rum flavoring, and orange juice.

4. Bake covered for 15 minutes.

(CONTINUED ON NEXT PAGE)

5. Test for tenderness with fork. (Use pot holders.) If not done, return to oven, lower heat to 300 degree F. and cook another 10 minutes.

MAKES 4 OR 6 SERVINGS

Note: If plantains are used, bake at 350 degrees F. for 45 minutes or until tender. Plantains can be bought year round in markets catering to Latin American and West Indian customers.

MAINE

Cape Neddick Light

POACHED COD

Codfish is very important to the economy of Maine. Poaching keeps the fish fluffy and sweet-tasting.

HERE'S WHAT YOU NEED:

1 pound cod fillets or steaks,
  fresh or frozen
1 tablespoon white vinegar
1 teaspoon onion salt

6 peppercorns
2 or 3 sprigs parsley or 1
  teaspoon dried parsley
3 or 4 cloves

HERE'S WHAT YOU DO:

1. Add water to fry pan to depth of 2 inches, enough to cover fillets.

2. Place on medium heat and bring to a boil.

3. Cut cod fillets in large serving pieces and put in fry pan.

4. Measure and add vinegar and onion salt. Sprinkle peppercorns, parsley, and cloves in water over fish.

5. Cover and lower heat once water has begun to boil again. Simmer gently for 10 minutes or until done. Cook fish only until it flakes easily with a fork. Do not overcook.

MAKES 4 SERVINGS

BREAD PUDDING

Spices were introduced to New England by crews of sailing vessels that left ports from Maine to Connecticut. Homemakers began to use them in everyday dishes like bread pudding.

HERE'S WHAT YOU NEED:

Softened butter   ¼ teaspoon ginger
4 slices white bread   ⅛ teaspoon salt
½ cup brown sugar   2 eggs
½ teaspoon nutmeg   2 cups milk
½ teaspoon cinnamon   Jam

HERE'S WHAT YOU DO:

1. Preheat oven to 325 degrees F. Butter 8×8-inch pan.

2. Butter bread and break up into small pieces. Place in baking dish.

3. Measure sugar, spices, and salt and mix together. Sprinkle over bread.

4. Beat eggs. Measure milk and combine with eggs. Pour over bread.

5. Bake about 30 minutes.

6. After taking from oven (use pot holders), spoon jam over top.

MAKES 4 SERVINGS

MARYLAND

The State House at Annapolis

MARYLAND STUFFED HAM

This famous Maryland dish was served to me by good friends. Even those of you who usually say "no" to greens, may like the spicy taste of this easier version.

HERE'S WHAT YOU NEED:

*1 package (10 ounces)
frozen chopped or leaf
spinach
1 package (10 ounces)
frozen kale or turnip greens
1 precooked smoked ham
slice (1½ inches thick,
about 2½ pounds)*

*5 or 6 stalks celery
1 teaspoon salt
¼ teaspoon black pepper
⅛ teaspoon red pepper
¼ teaspoon mustard seed
Dash of Tabasco sauce*

HERE'S WHAT YOU DO:

1. Open packages of greens so that they begin to thaw.

2. Trim fat off side of ham slice. Cut fat into small pieces, brown over medium heat in deep heavy fry pan. Remove bits of cooked fat.

3. While fat is frying, wash and slice celery. Cook in fry pan 2 to 3 minutes.

4. Mix spinach and kale with celery in fry pan. Carefully add total amount of water called for on packages.

5. Measure and sprinkle seasonings over greens. Cover and cook over medium heat until vegetables are tender, about 20 to 30 minutes.

6. Place ham slice on top of greens during last 15 minutes.

MAKES 6 TO 8 SERVINGS

STRAWBERRY FOOL

The word "fool," when used in cooking, means a dessert of mashed fruit mixed with cream. It is an old English dish and is popular in sections of America, such as Maryland, that were settled by the British.

HERE'S WHAT YOU NEED:

2 cups strawberries (or other
    berries)
½ cup sugar

½ cup water
1 cup whipped cream (see
    page 180)

HERE'S WHAT YOU DO:

1. Wash strawberries under running water. Remove stems and hulls. Cut into small pieces, and place in saucepan.

2. Measure sugar and sprinkle over fruit. Add ½ cup water. Bring to boil, lower heat, and cook for about 3 minutes. Stir now and then to keep fruit from sticking.

3. Drain cooked fruit through strainer and cool quickly in refrigerator or over bowl of ice.

4. Whip cream and fold into cooled fruit. Refrigerate for 1 or more hours. Spoon into tall parfait or sherbet glasses.

MAKES 4 SERVINGS

Note: You do not have to use whipped cream. If you prefer you may stir in ½ cup sweetened heavy cream.

MASSACHUSETTS

Old Ironsides, The USS Constitution, Boston

TOLLHOUSE COOKIES

A similar cookie was sold at tollhouse inns on the highway in early colonial times.

HERE'S WHAT YOU NEED:

¾ cup (1½ sticks) butter
¾ cup white sugar
¾ cup firmly packed brown
   sugar
1 egg
1 teaspoon vanilla
3 tablespoons milk
2½ cups sifted flour
1 teaspoon baking powder

¼ teaspoon salt
1 cup nuts (walnuts, pecans,
   filberts, or others of your
   choice)
1 package (12 ounces)
   semisweet chocolate pieces
Small amount of shortening
   to grease baking sheets

HERE'S WHAT YOU DO:

1. Place butter in bowl. Soften by beating with wooden spoon or electric mixer.

2. Measure and add sugars slowly, continuing to beat.

3. Break egg into separate small bowl. Measure and add vanilla and milk. Beat with egg beater. Stir into butter-sugar mixture. Mix thoroughly.

4. Sift flour, measure, and pour back into sifter. Measure and add baking powder and salt and sift again. Stir into batter.

5. Chop nuts and add nuts and chocolate pieces.

6. Preheat oven to 375 degrees F. Grease baking sheets.

7. Use two teaspoons and dip about half a teaspoon of dough onto one teaspoon. With the back of the other, scrape off onto baking sheet. Leave abut 1 inch between cookies.

74

8. Bake 8 to 10 minutes until golden, not dark brown.

9. Remove from oven and take cookies off sheet with spatula. Cool on cake rack.

MAKES 40 TO 50 COOKIES

CANDIED CRANBERRIES

Cranberries are an important farm crop in Massachusetts.

HERE'S WHAT YOU NEED:

1 cup cranberries
1 cup sugar
1 cup water

HERE'S WHAT YOU DO:

1. Wash and dry cranberries.

2. Prick each one in several places with fork.

3. Measure sugar and water and pour into saucepan. Place over medium heat and boil until syrup reaches 234 degrees F. Use a candy thermometer.

4. Add cranberries, and lower heat. Continue cooking until syrup jells and becomes thick when dropped from tip of spoon. (You may need some assistance from an older person.)

5. Remove berries with slotted spoon or fork. Drain thoroughly and cool on wax paper.

6. Place additional sugar on wax paper and roll cooled berries in it.

MAKES APPROXIMATELY 1 CUP

MICHIGAN

automotive center of america

CORNISH PASTIES

Little meat pies called "pasties" were introduced to Michigan a hundred years ago when men from Cornwall (southwest England) came to work in the iron mines. Pasties are great for today's picnics, hot or cold, as well as for meals at home.

HERE'S WHAT YOU NEED:

1 cup cooked beef, cut up
1 medium-size carrot
1 medium-size potato
¾ cup leftover or canned
gravy
1 teaspoon onion salt
1 package piecrust mix

HERE'S WHAT YOU DO:

1. Cut beef into very small pieces using paring knife.

2. Scrub carrot with vegetable brush under running water. Cut in thin rounds.

3. Peel and cut potato into small cubes.

4. Place beef, potato, carrot, and ¾ cup gravy in saucepan or fry pan over medium heat. Measure and sprinkle onion salt over mixture. Lower heat and simmer for 5 to 10 minutes. Remove to cool.

5. Prepare piecrust following instructions on package. Roll dough as thin as possible with rolling pin. Cut into 4-inch rounds with biscuit cutter or top of wide jar.

6. Preheat oven to 400 degrees F. Lightly grease baking sheet.

(CONTINUED ON NEXT PAGE)

77

7. Place 1 tablespoon of meat and vegetables (use as little gravy as possible) in center of round. Moisten edges of pastry rounds lightly with water to make them stick, and fold over. Press edges together with fork.

8. Place on baking sheet and bake for 10 to 12 minutes until brown.

MAKES 4 TO 6 SERVINGS

RHUBARB PARFAIT

Rhubarb, called "pie plant" by early settlers, is the first fresh fruit of the year. An annual rhubarb festival used to take place in the Pontiac, Michigan, area.

HERE'S WHAT YOU NEED:

1 pound fresh rhubarb	*1 cup sugar*
2 tablespoons quick-cooking tapioca	*1 cup whipped cream (see page 180)*
¼ cup water, approximately	*1 or 2 small bananas*

HERE'S WHAT YOU DO:

1. Wash rhubarb, remove leaves and stem ends. Peel only if stalks are not tender. Cut into 1-inch-long pieces.

2. Place in saucepan. Measure and sprinkle tapioca over rhubarb. Add small amount of water, about ¼ cup. Rhubarb has a considerable amount of water in it.

3. Cook over medium heat until almost tender. Add more water if needed so that it does not burn. Measure and stir in sugar and continue cooking until tender.

78

4. Remove from heat and cool.

5. Whip cream.

6. Peel and slice bananas.

7. Into tall parfait glasses, spoon layers of rhubarb, whipped cream, and sliced bananas, and top with whipped cream.

MAKES 4 SERVINGS

Note: If frozen rhubarb is used, follow instructions for cooking on package.

MINNESOTA

minor smooth waters

EASY DANISH DESSERT

Pioneer women not only took care of their homes and families, but frequently worked on the farm as well. An easy dish like this one was as welcome to them as it will be to you when you want to fix a quick delicious dessert.

HERE'S WHAT YOU NEED:

1 pound butter cookies
1 cup whipped cream (see page 180)
½ cup raspberry or strawberry preserves, or sweetened fresh
  berries

HERE'S WHAT YOU DO:

1. Crush cookies fine with rolling pin, enough for 1½ cups.

2. Whip cream.

3. Measure and add preserves and cookie crumbs to whipped cream. Stir gently until blended.

4. Spoon into sherbet or parfait dishes. May be eaten immediately or placed in refrigerator for several hours.

MAKES 4 TO 6 SERVINGS

NORWEGIAN MEAT BALLS

Half of the early settlers in Minnesota were from Scandinavian countries: Norway, Sweden, Denmark, and Finland. Many of their children and grandchildren still live in this state of blue lakes. The Scandinavian influence in home and restaurant cooking stays strong.

HERE'S WHAT YOU NEED:

1 small onion
1 tablespoon butter or
margarine
2 or 3 slices white bread,
enough to make ½ cup
crumbs
⅓ cup milk
1 egg

1 teaspoon salt
¼ teaspoon allspice
⅛ teaspoon pepper
1 pound ground
beef-pork-veal, usually
prepackaged as "meat loaf"
mixture

HERE'S WHAT YOU DO:

1. Peel and grate onion, enough for 2 tablespoons.

2. Melt butter in small fry pan and cook onion until soft, not brown.

3. Tear bread slices into ½ cup of small crumbs. Soak bread in ⅓ cup of milk while you continue with recipe.

4. Break egg into bowl. Measure and add salt, allspice, and pepper. Beat lightly with egg beater or fork.

5. Add meat, onions, and bread crumbs with milk. Mix thoroughly.

6. Preheat oven to 350 degrees F. Lightly grease shallow baking pan.

7. Shape meat mixture into balls, using a rounded tablespoon of mixture for each. Place in pan. Bake until done, about 18 minutes.

8. If you like gravy, follow instructions for Cream Gravy on page 89. Use sour cream instead of milk and add 1 teaspoon crushed dried dill.

MAKES ABOUT 25 MEAT BALLS

MISSISSIPPI

Dunleath Plantation House, Natchez

CUSTARD

A still popular dessert in the South is a soft boiled custard, often served as part of New Year's dinner. Its serving shows the influence of the early French colonists, whose rich custard was called *crème*.

HERE'S WHAT YOU NEED:

4 eggs   *2 cups milk*
¼ cup sugar   *½ teaspoon vanilla*
⅛ teaspoon salt

HERE'S WHAT YOU DO:

1. Fill lower part of double boiler with water. There should be enough so that the top part of the double boiler will rest about ½ inch above the water.

2. Put on high heat until water boils, and then lower to medium.

3. While water is beginning to heat, separate egg yolks from whites and put yolks into top of double boiler. (Egg whites can be refrigerated and used another time [see page 179]).

4. Measure and add sugar, salt, and milk to egg yolks. Beat lightly with egg beater.

5. Place top of double boiler on lower part. Stir custard constantly until mixture thickens. It is cooked when custard coats a metal spoon.

6. Remove from heat. Add vanilla. Cool slightly. Pour into sherbet dishes.

MAKES 4 TO 6 SERVINGS

Note: If you would like to save money, you can use ½ cup non-fat dry milk powder and 2 cups lukewarm water instead of milk.

85

FISH STEW

There's a lot of river and stream fishing in Mississippi. Fish stew suppers are very popular. The stew is frequently cooked out of doors in a large iron pot on an open wood fire. This is a good recipe for camping trips when fishing is included. Of course, you can prepare fish stew right in your own kitchen in a heavy fry pan.

HERE'S WHAT YOU NEED:

2 slices bacon
1 pound fresh (or frozen)
 boned fish
1 teaspoon onion salt

6 tablespoons catsup
2 cups milk
2 tablespoons flour
1 tablespoon salt

HERE'S WHAT YOU DO:

1. Cut bacon into small pieces and brown in iron pot over low outdoor fire.

2. Cut fish into serving pieces and add to hot bacon fat. Brown lightly. Measure and sprinkle onion salt over fish. Add catsup and 1 cup milk. Cook another 5 minutes.

3. While fish is cooking, mix 1 cup milk with 2 tablespoons flour and 1 tablespoon salt. Stir with fork to blend.

4. Add milk-flour combination slowly to fish stew. Bring to a boil until liquid is thickened.

MAKES 4 SERVINGS

Note: Another way of preparing fish stew is to add 2 cups canned tomatoes instead of milk.

MISSOURI

Broad farmlands

BISCUITS AND GRAVY

This is a favorite combination in Missouri and throughout the South.

BISCUITS

HERE'S WHAT YOU NEED:

2 cups unsifted flour
1 teaspoon salt
1 tablespoon baking powder

⅓ cup shortening
¾ cup milk

HERE'S WHAT YOU DO:

1. Preheat oven to 450 degrees F.

2. Measure flour, salt, and baking powder into mixing bowl. Blend.

3. Measure shortening and spoon into dry mixture. Mix with fork or pastry blender until crumbly.

4. Measure and add most of milk to dry ingredients. Mix only enough to blend, and handle lightly. Add more milk if needed. Dough should be soft but not sticky. Form dough into ball, and then flatten out with hand.

5. Knead dough on floured board ten to twelve times. To knead means to fold the ball of dough toward you. Then push the edges of the dough into each other and away from you with the palm of your hand. Turn dough once or twice.

6. Roll dough on wax paper with rolling pin to ½-inch thickness and cut with 2-inch cutter. Place on ungreased baking sheet.

7. Bake 12 to 15 minutes.

MAKES 12 BISCUITS

CREAM GRAVY

HERE'S WHAT YOU NEED:

*3 tablespoons bacon or
  sausage fat and crusty
  brown bits left after frying*

*2 tablespoons flour
1 cup milk
Salt and pepper*

HERE'S WHAT YOU DO:

1. Measure fat and drippings into fry pan over medium heat.

2. Measure flour and stir in until lightly browned.

3. Add milk slowly and mix. Cook until thick, continuing to stir. (Take off heat if gravy begins to lump and stir vigorously. Return to heat.)

4. Season with salt and pepper.

5. Pour over hot biscuits.

MAKES ABOUT 1 CUP GRAVY

WIGWAM PUDDING

This recipe came from a woman in Missouri who said that she had heard that I was looking for recipes from her state. She remembered that her grandmother always helped her make wigwam pudding. Here is her recipe, with instant pudding.

HERE'S WHAT YOU NEED:

1 package instant vanilla
  pudding
1 ¾ cups half-and-half cream

¼ cup sour cream
24 vanilla wafers
2 small peaches

HERE'S WHAT YOU DO:

1. Prepare pudding according to directions on the package using half-and-half cream instead of milk. After it thickens, stir in sour cream.

2. Crumble 2 or 3 vanilla wafers each into the bottom of four dessert dishes, enough to make thin layer.

3. Pour small amount of pudding over crumbs.

4. Wash, dry, remove seed, and slice peaches. Place on pudding.

5. Add a final layer of pudding.

6. Stand 3 vanilla wafers in wigwam fashion over pudding in each dish.

MAKES 4 SERVINGS

MONTANA

Two Medicine Lake

SENATE BEAN SOUP

This soup is served in the restaurants of the Capitol Building in Washington, D.C. A senator from Montana is said to have been the first to introduce the recipe.

One story says that in 1904 the Speaker of the House, Joseph Cannon of Illinois, came into the restaurant on a hot and muggy day and ordered bean soup. It was not on the menu because of the weather. "Thunderation," roared Speaker Cannon, "I had my mouth set for bean soup"; and, he continued, "From now on, hot or cold, rain, snow, or shine, I want it on the menu." And so it has been.

I have changed the recipe a little to make it easier for you.

HERE'S WHAT YOU NEED:

> 1 large cooked smoked ham
>   bone
> 1 pound dry white beans
> 2 onions

> 4 or 5 stalks celery, enough
>   for 1 cup
> 1 teaspoon garlic powder
> Salt and pepper

HERE'S WHAT YOU DO:

1. Place ham bone in large pot and cover with water. Bring to boil, lower heat, cover, and simmer for 1 hour.

2. Wash beans thoroughly (see page 180).

3. In another pot, cover beans with water. Bring to a boil. Remove from heat, and let stand while ham bone is simmering.

4. Peel onions and chop. Wash celery and chop.

5. Remove pot with ham bone from heat. Drain beans and add to ham along with onions, celery, and garlic powder.

6. Bring again to boil, lower heat, and simmer, covered, for 2 hours or until beans are soft.

7. Remove ham and bone. Cut off meat with paring knife on chopping board and return meat to soup. (You may need help.)

8. Add salt and pepper to taste. Mash some of the beans with spoon to thicken soup.

MAKES ABOUT 4 QUARTS

Note: Celery can be left out.

SCALLOPED CARROTS

People in Montana are proud of their home-grown potatoes and carrots.

HERE'S WHAT YOU NEED:

*Small amount of shortening
  to grease casserole
8 medium-size carrots
3 cups unflavored coarse
  bread crumbs*

*1 teaspoon salt
Dash of pepper
¼ pound Cheddar cheese or
  cheese of your choice
¾ or 1 cup milk, as needed*

HERE'S WHAT YOU DO:

1. Preheat oven to 350 degrees F. Grease large casserole.

2. Peel carrots with vegetable peeler. Grate on coarse side of grater and place in baking dish. Grate slowly so that your fingers will not slip.

3. Measure bread crumbs and mix with carrots. Season with salt and pepper.

(CONTINUED ON NEXT PAGE)

4. Grate cheese and sprinkle over top.

5. Add milk to cover mixture.

6. Bake for 1 hour. Remember to use pot holders.

MAKES 4 SERVINGS

NEBRASKA

Chimney Rock, landmark of the old Oregon Trail

RAISIN SOUR CREAM PIE

With a shortage of fresh fruit, pioneer women used dried fruits like raisins to give variety to winter menus. Raisin sour cream pie is still served in Nebraska, where it was my grandmother's favorite winter pie.

HERE'S WHAT YOU NEED:

2 eggs
½ cup sugar
1 cup raisins
1 cup sour cream

2 tablespoons flour
1 teaspoon vanilla
1 8-inch cereal pie shell (*see page 182*)

HERE'S WHAT YOU DO:

1. Preheat oven to 350 degrees F.

2. Separate eggs and put yolks in medium-size bowl (see page 179). (Egg whites should be stored in refrigerator and used for other recipes). Beat yolks lightly.

3. Measure and add sugar. Beat again until sugar is blended.

4. Measure and add raisins, sour cream, flour, and vanilla.

5. Mix and pour into cereal shell.

6. Place in oven and bake 30 minutes or until filling is set. Use pot holders. (Table knife inserted in center will come out clean when pie is done.)

MAKES 6 TO 8 SERVINGS

PORCUPINE MEAT BALLS

The name comes from the fact that the rice looks like porcupine quills in these meat balls. The recipe is popular in cattle-raising Nebraska with its plentiful beef supply because ranch and farm families welcome variety in the way they serve ground beef.

HERE'S WHAT YOU NEED:

*Small amount of shortening
to grease casserole
1 pound ground beef
½ cup uncooked rice
1 teaspoon onion salt*

*⅛ teaspoon pepper
⅛ teaspoon nutmeg
1 can (11 ounces) tomato
soup
½ cup water*

HERE'S WHAT YOU DO:

1. Preheat oven to 350 degrees F. Lightly grease medium casserole.

2. Place ground beef in mixing bowl. Measure and add rice, onion salt, pepper, and nutmeg. Mix thoroughly.

3. Form into small balls, about 1½ inches. Place in casserole.

4. Mix tomato soup with water. Pour over meat.

5. Bake covered about 1 hour.

6. Cover may be removed during last 15 minutes of baking to allow meat to brown. (Use pot holders.)

MAKES 8 SERVINGS

NEVADA

Wide open spaces

PIÑON NUT SUNFLOWER CAKES

Piñon nuts are the seeds in the pine cones of certain evergreen trees. Western Indians, including Washoes, Paiutes, and Shoshones, value the nuts as an important food.

The traditional Indian way of cooking these cakes is to roll them in leaves and bake in warm ashes. The cakes can be eaten with other foods, or crumbled into stews or soups.

HERE'S WHAT YOU NEED:

½ cup raw sunflower seeds (shelled)
½ cup raw piñon nuts (shelled)
Salt

HERE'S WHAT YOU DO:

1. Preheat oven to 350 degrees F.

2. Measure and grind seeds and nuts in blender (with adult help), or food grinder.

3. Sprinkle lightly with salt and form flat small cakes, 2 tablespoons per cake.

4. Wrap each cake in aluminum foil and bake for about 50 minutes. Cakes should not get too brown.

MAKES 8 CAKES

Note: Sunflower seeds and piñon nuts (sometimes called pignolias) can be purchased in many supermarkets and in specialty or health food stores.

BEAN CASSEROLE

The Basques came from Spain to Nevada when it was first settled. Their main occupation, then and now, is sheep herding.

Like other immigrants, the Basques brought food customs with them: nourishing, sturdy food for men away in the hills and mountains for days at a time. Such food included sourdough bread, cheese, and baked white beans.

HERE'S WHAT YOU NEED:

1 pound washed dry white
beans (see page 180)
2 or 3 medium-size onions
¼ pound lean salt pork
2 teaspoons salt
1 teaspoon garlic salt
2 cups water
Small amount of shortening
to grease casserole

HERE'S WHAT YOU DO:

1. Place beans in large pot and cover with water. Bring to a boil for 2 minutes. Cover pan and let stand for 1 hour off heat.

2. Peel onions and slice in quarters.

3. Cut salt pork into small pieces.

4. Preheat oven to 300 degrees F. Grease deep casserole.

5. Drain beans through strainer and place in casserole. (You may need some help on this step.)

6. Add onions, salt pork, salt, and garlic salt to beans, and mix. Pour 2 cups of water over beans.

7. Cover and bake for 3 hours, or until beans are tender. Add more water if needed. (Use pot holders.)

Note: If you are camping, cook as the Basques sometimes still do. Prepare beans as above and place in a heavy Dutch oven. Bury the covered pot in the coals of the fire to cook all day or all night.

NEW HAMPSHIRE

smooth slopes

RED FLANNEL HASH

Families in New Hampshire, like their neighbors in the other New England states, have a heritage of making the most of leftover food. The following recipe gets its name from the red coloring of the beets and is prepared from leftover corned beef roast.

HERE'S WHAT YOU NEED:

*2 tablespoons butter,
margarine, or meat
drippings
1 cup cooked corned beef,
cut up (canned corned beef
may be used)*

*1 cup cooked beets, chopped
3 cups cooked potatoes,
chopped
1 teaspoon onion salt
½ cup beef broth or
consommé*

HERE'S WHAT YOU DO:

1. Place fry pan over medium heat and melt butter.

2. Cut up corned beef, chop beets and potatoes with paring knife on cutting board.

3. Spoon into fry pan. Sprinkle with onion salt.

4. Measure and add beef broth. Press beef and vegetables together with spatula.

5. Brown about 20 minutes, turning beef and vegetables several times.

MAKES 4 TO 6 SERVINGS

EASY RECIPE

DANDELION SALAD

When the settlers arrived in New Hampshire and other New England states, they were probably glad to see the familiar dandelion. They used it in their menus just as many Americans do today.

Dandelion leaves should be gathered in the spring before the plant flowers while the leaves are tender.

HERE'S WHAT YOU NEED:

2 cups dandelion leaves
1 small red onion
2 tomatoes

⅛ teaspoon basil
Salad dressing (see page 183)

HERE'S WHAT YOU DO:

1. Wash dandelion leaves well. Throw away damaged leaves. Chill in ice water while you continue with recipe.

2. Slice onion very thin.

3. Cut tomatoes in quarters.

4. Drain leaves through strainer. Dry with paper towel and tear into bite-size pieces. Place in salad bowl.

5. Add onion and tomatoes.

6. Sprinkle with basil and toss with salad dressing.

MAKES 4 SERVINGS

NEW JERSEY

Harvesting cucumbers

BLUEBERRY SAUCE

New Jersey, the Garden State, grows a wide variety of vegetables and fruits. Among those produced in abundance are peaches, strawberries, and blueberries.

HERE'S WHAT YOU NEED:

2 cups fresh blueberries
⅓ cup brown sugar

⅛ teaspoon salt
½ teaspoon lemon extract

HERE'S WHAT YOU DO:

1. Wash berries and place in medium saucepan.

2. Measure and add sugar and salt.

3. Place saucepan over medium to high heat. Bring to boil, lower heat immediately, and simmer for 2 or 3 minutes, no longer.

4. Remove from heat. Measure and stir in lemon extract. (Vanilla may be substituted.) Cool.

Serve over puddings, cakes, ice cream, and cereal.

MAKES 1½ CUPS

FRIED TOMATO SLICES

New Jersey tomatoes are famous for their flavor and size.

HERE'S WHAT YOU NEED:

3 large or 6 small tomatoes,
not too ripe
½ cup flour
1 teaspoon salt

⅛ teaspoon pepper
½ teaspoon sugar
¼ cup (½ stick) butter

HERE'S WHAT YOU DO:

1. Slice tomatoes ½ inch thick.

2. Measure and mix thoroughly: flour, salt, pepper, and sugar.

3. Melt butter in large fry pan over medium heat, enough to cover bottom of pan.

4. Dip tomato slices on each side in flour mixture. Fry until brown. Turn and brown other side.

MAKES 4 SERVINGS

HERO SANDWICHES

You can see the influence of Italian-Americans on food in New Jersey. Hero sandwiches, sometimes called "hoagies" or "grinders," are sold throughout the state.

HERE'S WHAT YOU NEED:

4 short loaves Italian bread or crusty rolls
¼ cup olive oil
¼ cup vinegar
½ teaspoon oregano
½ pound each salami, bologna, or other cold cuts

½ pound sliced Italian cheese (provolone or cheese of your choice)
Italian peppers (may be omitted)

HERE'S WHAT YOU DO:

1. Slice bread in half lengthwise with bread knife. (You may need help on the slicing.)

2. Measure oil, vinegar, and oregano. Mix thoroughly.

3. Sprinkle each bread slice lightly with oil and vinegar.

4. Layer one slice of meat, cheese, and another slice of meat on lower half of bread. Repeat layers.

5. Add drained Italian peppers.

6. Top with remaining crusty slice of bread.

MAKES 4 SERVINGS

Note: Shredded lettuce, chopped onion, and thinly sliced tomato may be added. Do not make sandwiches in advance. They become soggy.

NEW MEXICO

The Spanish mission church, Ranches of Taos

ROASTED PUMPKIN SEEDS

The Apache Indians traditionally held a special ceremony to ask for a bountiful harvest of pumpkins, an important food. A young boy was sent into the woods to gather berries from the blue juniper trees. On his return, he was blindfolded and sent into the pumpkin patch to scatter the berries far and wide. This, everyone hoped, would make for a plentiful pumpkin crop.

HERE'S WHAT YOU NEED:

1 pumpkin
Vegetable oil
Salt

HERE'S WHAT YOU DO:

1. Let an adult cut off the top of the pumpkin for you.

2. Remove the seeds and pulp of the pumpkin. (Pulp may be used in pie or other baked desserts.) Dry seeds in sunny window for several days, or in low oven (250 degrees F.) for several hours.

3. After seeds are dry, place in bowl and sprinkle vegetable oil over them lightly. Use as little oil as possible. Add salt and stir with mixing spoon or fork.

4. Spread oiled seeds on baking sheet. If you have not used oven, place baking sheet in oven and heat to 250 degrees F. Bake seeds, stirring now and then, until light brown. Do not let them get too brown. (Remember to use pot holders.)

Eat like salted nuts.

RANCH-STYLE EGGS
(*Huevos Rancheros*)

These ranch-style eggs show the influence of Spanish and Mexican cooking.

HERE'S WHAT YOU NEED:

2 tablespoons vegetable oil
1 or 2 green chili peppers or
  ¼ teaspoon chili powder
1 small onion
⅛ teaspoon garlic powder

½ teaspoon oregano
1 can (8 ounces) tomato
  sauce
Salt and pepper
4 eggs

HERE'S WHAT YOU DO:

1. Heat oil in large fry pan.

2. Cut green chili into small pieces. Fry on medium heat until pepper softens.

3. Chop onion on cutting board. Add to chili and fry until golden.

4. Measure and add garlic powder, oregano, and tomato sauce. Simmer about 5 minutes. Salt and pepper to taste.

5. Break whole eggs into sauce. Cover and cook until done.

MAKES 4 SERVINGS

Note: If fresh chili peppers are unavailable, use canned chilies (see page 11). They should be mashed and strained.

NEW YORK

Manhattan from Central Park

SENECA INDIAN STEW

Seneca Stew was a traditional dish of the northeastern Indians. They frequently ate boiled combinations of meats, vegetables, spices, and fruits obtained in trade with the colonists.

HERE'S WHAT YOU NEED:

½ cup flour
1 teaspoon salt
⅛ teaspoon pepper
2 pounds stewing beef
  (venison was used by the
  Indians)
2 medium onions
1 lemon

6 cloves
¼ cup raisins
¼ cup mincemeat
½ cup vegetable oil or
  shortening
⅓ cup water
1 can (1 pound) red kidney
  beans

HERE'S WHAT YOU DO:

1. Measure flour, salt, and pepper and mix together.

2. Roll pieces of beef in seasoned flour.

3. Chop onions. Remove several thin pieces of peel from lemon. Measure raisins and mincemeat.

4. Melt enough shortening to cover bottom of large heavy fry pan or Dutch oven over medium to high heat.

5. Fry meat until brown on all sides.

6. Add onions, lemon peel, cloves, raisins, mincemeat, and water.

7. Cover and simmer for 1½ hours.

8. Add kidney beans and heat.

MAKES 4 TO 6 SERVINGS

CHEESECAKE

Cheesecake is a popular dessert in New York City. Here is a no-cook version.

HERE'S WHAT YOU NEED:

1 8-inch crumb pie shell (see page 181)
1 package (8 ounces) cream cheese
2 cups half-and-half cream
1 package (3 ounces) lemon instant pudding mix
6 or 8 small strawberries

HERE'S WHAT YOU DO:

1. Prepare crumb pie shell.

2. Place cream cheese in bowl and stir with fork or wooden spoon until soft.

3. Add ½ cup of cream, blending until smooth.

4. Add remaining cream and pudding mix. Beat with egg beater until well mixed, about 2 minutes.

5. Pour into pie shell. Place in refrigerator to chill.

6. Just before serving, garnish with strawberries.

MAKES 8 SERVINGS

Note: Frozen strawberries, almost defrosted, can be used.

COLESLAW

The Dutch colonists introduced coleslaw, or cabbage salad, which is still popular all over the United States.

HERE'S WHAT YOU NEED:

1 small head cabbage
1 green pepper
½ cup mayonnaise
2 tablespoons cider vinegar

1 teaspoon onion salt
½ teaspoon celery seed
1 teaspoon sugar
⅛ teaspoon pepper

HERE'S WHAT YOU DO:

1. Remove outer leaves of cabbage. Cut in half. (Ask for help on this step if you need it.) Remove hard inner core. Grate cabbage on coarse side of grater or chop fine.

2. Wash and drain through a strainer. If cabbage is not crisp, soak in ice water for 10 to 15 minutes and drain again.

3. Wash green pepper and chop. Add to drained cabbage.

4. Measure mayonnaise in 1 cup measuring cup. Measure and add vinegar, onion salt, celery seed, sugar, and pepper. Blend.

5. Mix drained cabbage with dressing.

MAKES 6 TO 8 SERVINGS

Note: Other salad dressings may be used.

NORTH CAROLINA

Orton Plantation near Wilmington

APPLE MUFFINS

In North Carolina, where there's an annual Apple Festival in Lincoln County, this recipe was a winner.

HERE'S WHAT YOU NEED:

TOPPING

½ cup pecans
2 tablespoons brown sugar
½ teaspoon cinnamon

BATTER

2 cups flour
⅓ cup sugar
1 tablespoon baking powder
1 teaspoon salt
1½ teaspoons cinnamon

1 egg
¾ cup milk
3 tablespoons vegetable oil
1 medium-size cooking apple

HERE'S WHAT YOU DO:

1. Measure and chop pecans.

2. Measure and mix brown sugar and ½ teaspoon cinnamon with nuts. Put aside while you prepare batter.

3. Preheat oven to 400 degrees F.

4. Measure and mix flour, sugar, baking powder, salt, and cinnamon.

5. Break egg into bowl. Measure and add milk and vegetable oil. Beat with egg beater.

6. Wash and grate unpeeled apple and add to egg and milk.

(CONTINUED ON NEXT PAGE)

7. Add liquid to dry ingredients, stirring enough to moisten. Do not beat.

8. Grease muffin pans, or use paper liners in pans. Fill two thirds full with batter.

9. Sprinkle topping over each muffin and bake for 30 to 35 minutes.

MAKES 12 MUFFINS

SAUSAGE BALLS

Pork is a very popular meat in North Carolina. Try these sausage balls, which are highly seasoned and delicious.

HERE'S WHAT YOU NEED:

*½ pound spicy bulk pork
  sausage
4 ounces grated cheese*

*1 ¾ cups biscuit mix
¼ teaspoon thyme
⅛ teaspoon ginger*

HERE'S WHAT YOU DO:

1. Preheat oven to 350 degrees F.

2. Measure and mix ingredients together. Form into small balls, about 1½ inches.

3. Place in large shallow baking dish and bake for 20 minutes.

MAKES 25 TO 30 SAUSAGE BALLS

118

NORTH DAKOTA

migrating ducks

BERRY BUTTER

Early settlers in North Dakota found many kinds of berries growing wild. Today, gooseberries, raspberries, and strawberries still grow wild but are also cultivated in the gardens of North Dakota families.

This berry butter is delicious on toast or muffins.

HERE'S WHAT YOU NEED:

3 tablespoons fresh berries
1 tablespoon honey or sugar
*1 teaspoon bottled lemon
    juice*

*½ cup (1 stick) softened
    butter*

HERE'S WHAT YOU DO:

1. Wash berries and drain through strainer.

2. Place in small bowl and crush with fork. Stir in honey and lemon juice.

3. If butter is not completely softened, place in bowl and beat with mixing spoon. Blend in berry mixture.

MAKES ¾ CUP

HONEY SALAD DRESSING

Beekeeping is an important industry in North Dakota, where record crops of honey and beeswax are produced.

This salad dressing goes well over fruits like the Grapefruit and Melon Salad from Arizona.

HERE'S WHAT YOU NEED:

1 package (3 ounces)
  whipped cream cheese
½ teaspoon salt
1 tablespoon honey

⅛ teaspoon cayenne pepper
¼ teaspoon cinnamon
¼ cup orange juice
1 tablespoon lemon juice

HERE'S WHAT YOU DO:

1. Place cream cheese in medium-size bowl.

2. Measure and add salt, honey, cayenne, and cinnamon. Mix thoroughly.

3. Measure and add fruit juices slowly and stir until smooth.

MAKES ABOUT ¾ CUP

121

BANNOCK

Bannock is an easy-to-make bread enjoyed by early explorers, trappers, and Indians in North Dakota. It's handy for today's campers because it can be baked on a griddle or in a fry pan.

HERE'S WHAT YOU NEED:

3 cups flour
2 teaspoons baking powder
1 teaspoon salt

3 tablespoons milk
2 tablespoons vegetable oil or melted fat

HERE'S WHAT YOU DO:

1. Measure and mix flour, baking powder, and salt.

2. Add milk and oil.

3. Grease fry pan and spread dough in pan. Cover with cloth and place near campfire for about half an hour.

4. Cook on back of fire for 25 to 30 minutes, or until a toothpick placed in center comes out clean.

MAKES 6 SERVINGS

Note: Raisins, brown sugar, or dried berries may be added before baking to make a sweet bannock.
Dry milk may be used. Follow instructions for amount of water needed.

OHIO

Tractoring

HONEY NUT BARS

This cookie recipe comes from the annual Swiss Festival in Sugarcreek, Ohio, held in honor of the Swiss who founded the town.

HERE'S WHAT YOU NEED:

*Small amount of shortening
to grease pan
1½ cups flour
1 cup brown sugar
½ teaspoon baking powder
¼ teaspoon allspice
⅛ teaspoon nutmeg*

*2 eggs
½ cup honey
2 tablespoons butter or
margarine
2 ounces mixed candied fruit
½ cup nuts*

HERE'S WHAT YOU DO:

1. Preheat oven to 375 degrees F. Grease 11×7-inch baking pan.

2. Measure flour, sugar, baking powder, allspice, and nutmeg. Mix together in bowl.

3. Set aside about ¼ cup flour mixture.

4. Break eggs into another bowl. Beat lightly. Measure and pour in honey.

5. Melt butter in small pan on medium heat and blend in eggs slowly. Pour egg mixture into dry ingredients, stirring until smooth.

6. Chop candied fruit and nuts. Sprinkle with remaining flour mixture. Stir both into batter.

7. Spread in baking pan and bake for 30 to 40 minutes. May be served plain, or frosted. Cut in squares.

MAKES 40 SERVINGS

FRIED APPLES

"Johnny Appleseed" (John Chapman), the story says, went through the state planting apple seeds, dreaming of fine orchards. And fine orchards did grow in Ohio, where apples are served in many ways. When fried, they are eaten as a side dish with meat, possibly the influence of early German settlers.

HERE'S WHAT YOU NEED:

2 tablespoons bacon fat or
butter (enough to cover
bottom of fry pan)

3 red apples (any variety)
1 tablespoon brown sugar
1 tablespoon cider vinegar

HERE'S WHAT YOU DO:

1. Melt bacon fat in fry pan over medium heat.

2. Slice apples in half with paring knife. Remove core, and slice so that you have eight pieces per apple.

3. Fry slices in bacon fat for 3 or 4 minutes. Sprinkle with brown sugar and vinegar. Cover and fry 2 or 3 minutes longer, or until tender.

MAKES 4 SERVINGS

OKLAHOMA

The big farm

BAKED FUDGE CUSTARD

This dessert recipe was given to me by friends in Oklahoma. It was developed by Gladys Scivally, who was at one time director of the executive dining room for a large bank in Tulsa.

HERE'S WHAT YOU NEED:

*Small amount of shortening
to grease pan
4 eggs
2 cups sugar
½ cup flour*

*½ cup cocoa
1 cup (2 sticks) butter
2 teaspoons vanilla
1 cup nuts (any variety)*

HERE'S WHAT YOU DO:

1. Preheat oven to 325 degrees F. and lightly grease 8×10-inch baking pan.

2. Break eggs into bowl and beat.

3. Measure sugar, flour, and cocoa. Stir to blend.

4. Add gradually to eggs, beating all the time.

5. Melt butter in small saucepan and stir into batter.

6. Measure and add vanilla.

7. Chop nuts. Add to batter and mix lightly.

8. Pour into baking dish. Place dish in larger pan of hot water. Bake on middle rack in oven 45 to 60 minutes, or until firm like custard.

Serve with whipped cream (see page 180).

MAKES 10 TO 12 SERVINGS

NASTURTIUM SALAD

In the Plains states like Oklahoma, Indians made the most of the flowering nasturtium plant wherever it grew wild. When white settlers came, they named it "Indian cress" after the greens they were familiar with.

HERE'S WHAT YOU NEED:

*1 cup young nasturtium
   leaves*
⅓ cup vegetable oil
¼ cup vinegar
1 tablespoon honey
½ teaspoon salt

⅛ teaspoon pepper
*½ head iceberg or Boston
   lettuce*
*1 or 2 spring onions
   (scallions)*

HERE'S WHAT YOU DO:

1. Wash nasturtium leaves and chill in ice water for 5 minutes.

2. Prepare salad dressing by measuring oil, vinegar, honey, salt, and pepper into a jar. Close lid tightly and shake.

3. Drain nasturtium leaves and pat dry. Tear leaves and lettuce into bite-size pieces. Place in salad bowl.

4. Chop spring onions very fine on wooden cutting board with paring knife. Add to salad bowl along with greens. Shake dressing again (because honey settles), and sprinkle lightly over salad. Toss and serve.

MAKES 4 SERVINGS

Note: Parsley or water cress may be used instead of nasturtiums.

OREGON

Lost Lake and Mount Hood

FILBERT CHEESE WAFERS

Oregon grows 96 per cent of the nation's filbert nuts and so they are used a great deal in cooking.

HERE'S WHAT YOU NEED:

½ cup filbert nuts
½ cup (1 stick) butter or
   margarine, softened
1 glass (5 ounces) Old
   English sharp cheese

1¼ cups flour
½ teaspoon salt
⅛ teaspoon cayenne pepper

HERE'S WHAT YOU DO:

1. Chop filberts fine with paring knife on wooden chopping board.

2. Mix butter and cheese.

3. Measure flour, salt, and pepper. Blend together. (Be exact about the pepper; it's hot.)

4. Combine butter mixture and flour mixture to make dough.

5. Form dough into long roll, about 1½ inches in diameter. Wrap in transparent plastic wrap and refrigerate for several hours, or place in freezer for 10 to 15 minutes.

6. Preheat oven to 375 degrees F.

7. Slice roll into thin circles, and bake for approximately 12 minutes, on ungreased baking sheet.

MAKES ABOUT 75 SMALL WAFERS

Note: The filbert is also known as a hazelnut.

QUICK STRAWBERRY SHORTCAKE

The shortcake served at the annual Strawberry Festival in Lebanon, Oregon, is 16 feet long, 12 feet wide, and 8 feet high, and weighs over 5,700 pounds.

Here is an easier recipe for you and your friends.

HERE'S WHAT YOU NEED:

1 pint fresh strawberries *1 cup whipped cream (see*
¼ cup sugar *page 180)*
4 spongecake shells

HERE'S WHAT YOU DO:

1. Wash strawberries gently before using. Do not soak in water. Remove stems and hulls.

2. Drain thoroughly, slice berries and sprinkle with ¼ cup sugar.

3. Divide among four cake shells.

4. Prepare whipped cream and spoon over berries.

MAKES 4 SERVINGS

131

PENNSYLVANIA

Independence Hall, Philadelphia

PENNSYLVANIA DUTCH FUNNEL CAKES

Mennonites, Amish, and other religious groups, known collectively as Pennsylvania Dutch, settled in Lancaster Valley. The customs and life style of those settlers have been continued by many of their descendants.

HERE'S WHAT YOU NEED:

1 egg
⅔ cup milk
1 ⅓ cups flour
2 tablespoons sugar

¼ teaspoon salt
¾ teaspoon baking powder
Shortening

HERE'S WHAT YOU DO:

1. Break egg into medium-size bowl and add milk. Beat lightly.

2. Measure flour in 2-cup measuring cup. Measure and add sugar, salt, and baking powder. Stir gently.

3. Mix dry ingredients with egg and milk. Beat until smooth.

4. Place deep fry pan over medium to high heat with enough shortening to fill the pan half full. (An electric fry pan is useful.) Temperature should be 375 degrees F.

5. Hold finger of one hand over the spout of a funnel, pour batter into funnel with other hand. Remove finger and allow batter to drop gently into fat, swirling into circles from center out to about 3 inches.

6. Fry until golden. Remove with slotted spoon and drain on brown paper.

Serve plain or sprinkled with confectioners' sugar.

MAKES 10 CAKES, DEPENDING UPON SIZE

CHOCOLATE VELVET DESSERT

If you are near the town of Hershey, Pennsylvania, you can visit the chocolate factory there.

HERE'S WHAT YOU NEED:

⅔ cup chocolate-flavored
  syrup
⅔ cup sweetened condensed
  milk

½ teaspoon vanilla
⅓ cup wheat germ
2 cups whipped cream (*see page 180*)

HERE'S WHAT YOU DO:

1. Measure and mix together syrup, condensed milk, vanilla, and wheat germ.

2. Whip cream until very stiff but do not include sugar.

3. Gently fold whipped cream into chocolate mixture.

4. Spoon into ice cube trays and place in freezer.

5. Freeze until firm.

MAKES 4 TO 6 SERVINGS

134

RHODE ISLAND

Rock wall near Tiverton

RHODE ISLAND JOHNNYCAKES

This bread was originally named journey cake, because it was a favorite with travelers. Today it is spelled jonnycake or johnnycake and is prepared and served in many different ways. Here is one version.

HERE'S WHAT YOU NEED:

1 cup white corn meal
1 teaspoon salt
1 teaspoon sugar

1¼ cups boiling water
Small amount of shortening
to grease pan

HERE'S WHAT YOU DO:

1. Measure and mix corn meal, salt, and sugar.

2. Add boiling water gradually to make a thick batter.

3. Grease griddle with shortening and place on medium to high heat.

4. Pour ¼ cup of batter on griddle for each cake. Bake cakes on one side until golden brown; turn and bake on other side.

Serve with butter, or butter and syrup.

MAKES 12 CAKES

Note: Molasses may be used instead of sugar; milk instead of water, or along with water.

CRANBERRY-ORANGE PUNCH

Some Indian tribes called this native American fruit *Sassamanesh,* while others called it *Atoqua.* It is the familiar cranberry, now grown commercially in many states, including Rhode Island.

HERE'S WHAT YOU NEED:

1 quart cranberry juice cocktail
1 quart orange juice

4 or 6 ice cubes
½ pint lemon sherbet

HERE'S WHAT YOU DO:

1. Combine the juices in a large pitcher or punch bowl. Add 4 to 6 ice cubes and mix.

2. Just before serving, stir in lemon sherbet.

MAKES 8 TO 12 SERVINGS

Note: You can make an individual fruit drink by mixing ½ glass of cranberry juice with ½ glass of orange juice and a scoopful of lemon sherbet.

SOUTH CAROLINA

Cotton Picker

SESAME BAR COOKIES

Sesame seeds were brought to South Carolina in colonial times by African slaves. If they're not available in your area, substitute any finely chopped nuts.

HERE'S WHAT YOU NEED:

¼ cup sesame seeds
1 cup (2 sticks) butter or
   margarine
1 cup brown sugar
1 egg

1 teaspoon vanilla
1¾ cups flour
¼ teaspoon cinnamon
¼ teaspoon allspice
½ cup nuts

HERE'S WHAT YOU DO:

1. Preheat oven to 350 degrees F. Lightly grease an approximately 8×13-inch baking dish.

2. Place sesame seeds on foil in a smaller shallow baking dish and toast until golden, about 15 minutes.

3. Place butter in mixing bowl and beat to soften. Measure and slowly add brown sugar. Mix until blended.

4. Add egg and vanilla. Mix well.

5. Measure flour into 2-cup measuring cup. Measure and stir in spices.

6. Chop nuts on cutting board with paring knife.

7. Add flour slowly to creamed mixture, beating continuously until smooth.

8. Fold in nuts and sesame seeds.

(CONTINUED ON NEXT PAGE)

9. Spoon into baking dish and level with spatula or table knife. Bake 20 minutes.

10. Cut into bars while still warm.

MAKES ABOUT 48 PIECES

HOPPING JOHN
(Rice and Peas)

This was a favorite in early colonial times and still is. The recipe is inexpensive and can be made from leftovers.

HERE'S WHAT YOU NEED:

1 cup dry black-eyed peas *Butter*
¼ pound salt pork or bacon *Salt and pepper*
1 cup cooked rice

HERE'S WHAT YOU DO:

1. Wash dry peas (see page 180).

2. Measure peas into heavy saucepan and cover with water. Add salt pork. Bring to a boil, cover, and cook until tender, about 1½ hours. There should be only a small amount of liquid left. If too much, drain.

3. Mix cooked rice and peas together. Heat. Season with butter, salt, and pepper.

MAKES 4 SERVINGS

Note: Soak black-eyed peas overnight for faster cooking. (Black-eyed peas can also be bought canned or frozen.)

SOUTH DAKOTA

The Badlands

WHEAT GARDEN SALAD
(*Tabooley*)

Among the wave of settlers to the Midwest, there were only a few immigrants from Syria, Armenia, and Lebanon. However, these energetic strangers frequently owned the single grocery store in frontier settlements. They carried with them different ways of using our everyday foods. This recipe for *Tabooley* was brought to Deadwood, a roaring mining town, from Lebanon by Mr. and Mrs. George Shama, pioneer grocers.

Middle Eastern cooking is especially interesting today to people who like natural foods.

HERE'S WHAT YOU NEED:

1 cup finely ground cracked
    wheat (bulgur)
3 or 4 scallions or 1 small
    sweet onion
1 cup fresh parsley
½ cup fresh mint

4 medium tomatoes
2 lemons, enough for ½ cup
    juice
½ cup olive oil
Salt

HERE'S WHAT YOU DO:

1. Wash cracked wheat as you would dry beans (see page 180). Drain dry, fluffing now and then with fork, in fine strainer.

2. Wash scallions and cut off root tip. Chop whole scallion.

3. Wash parsley and mint. Pat dry with towel. Cut into small pieces with kitchen scissors or with paring knife, enough for 1 cup parsley and ½ cup mint.

4. Wash tomatoes and dry. Cut into bite-size pieces.

5. Spoon wheat into large bowl. Stir in vegetables, parsley, and mint.

6. To make salad dressing, squeeze juice from lemons (enough to make ½ cup) and combine with ½ cup olive oil.

7. Sprinkle dressing over wheat and vegetables. Mix lightly with fork. Salt to taste. (Pepper is not used because the flavor is delicate.)

8. Cover and refrigerate for an hour (2 or 3 hours is even better) to let flavors blend.

MAKES 4 TO 6 SERVINGS

143

RODEO HAMBURGERS

"The Days of '76" rodeo in Deadwood, South Dakota, is one of the outstanding rodeos in the country. It is complete with exciting contests, parades, and carnivals.

What I remember best, however, is the taste of hamburgers grilled on the midway.

HERE'S WHAT YOU NEED:

1 pound ground hamburger   *Salt and pepper*
  beef, chuck or round steak   *4 hamburger rolls*
Small amount of shortening

HERE'S WHAT YOU DO:

1. Divide hamburger into four equal parts. Shape into flat patties.

2. Rub fry pan lightly with shortening and place over medium to high heat.

3. Place patties in pan and brown on one side. Turn and brown on other side.

4. Immediately lower heat and continue cooking until done, 5 minutes more for rare; 10 for medium, and 12 minutes for well done.

5. Season with salt and pepper and serve on rolls.

MAKES 4 SERVINGS

TENNESSEE

The Great Smoky Mountains

DRIED APPLES

Apples are grown in many of our states, including Tennessee. People in that southern state frequently dry apples to preserve their home-grown crop. The drying process is a natural method of preserving foods.

HERE'S WHAT YOU NEED:

Ripe firm apples
3 tablespoons salt
2 quarts water

HERE'S WHAT YOU DO:

1. Wash, peel, and core apples. Cut apples into thin slices or circles.

2. Mix 3 tablespoons salt with 2 quarts water. Drop slices into salted water. Let stand 10 to 15 minutes.

3. Lift apple slices out of water and drain.

4. Place apples on drying racks, baking sheets, or spread on a large clean cloth. Make single layers for quick and even drying.

FOR SUN DRYING:

1. Place outside on a table high off the ground or on a porch roof. To protect from dirt and animals, cover with a screen or thin clean cloth.

2. Turn apples occasionally.

3. Bring them in each day before sundown. Keep fruit from getting wet.

4. Dry in the sun for 3 to 5 days, depending on heat of sun and moisture in air. Fruit is dry when it feels leathery.

FOR OVEN DRYING:

1. Preheat oven to 150 degrees F.

2. Place racks or baking sheets in the oven. Leave space around them for air to circulate.

3. Prop oven door open slightly to allow moisture to escape.

4. Dry for about 12 hours.

HOMINY GRITS

Grits, one of our oldest foods, have been eaten since people first grew and ground corn into meal.

Today grits are eaten mostly in our southern states. They are served at breakfast or at other meals as a substitute for potatoes.

HERE'S WHAT YOU NEED:

4 cups water   *¾ teaspoon salt*
1 cup hominy grits   *Butter*

HERE'S WHAT YOU DO:

1. Measure and pour water into 1½-quart saucepan.

2. Bring to boil over high heat.

3. Pour grits slowly into boiling water. Stir until mixture boils. Lower heat immediately. Add salt, cover, and simmer 1 hour or according to instructions on package, stirring frequently.

4. When ready to serve, top with a pat of butter.

MAKES 4 TO 6 SERVINGS

TEXAS

The Alamo, San Antonio

BARBECUE SAUCE

In a state as big as Texas, there are many types of food served. But everywhere in Texas, you will find barbecuing, much of it done in trenches in the ground. Recipes for sauces are many and varied. This is a simple one, but delicious.

HERE'S WHAT YOU NEED:

2 cups catsup
⅔ cup Worcestershire sauce
½ cup vinegar

1 teaspoon garlic salt
⅛ teaspoon cayenne pepper
2 tablespoons vegetable oil

HERE'S WHAT YOU DO:

1. Measure and pour all ingredients into saucepan.

2. Place on medium to high heat and bring to a boil. Lower heat immediately and simmer for 20 minutes.

MAKES 3½ CUPS

Note: Keep refrigerated when not using.

150

SCALLOPED SWEET POTATOES

When we think of Texas, we often think of western and Mexican dishes. But there is a southern influence on Texas cooking as well. Here is a sweet potato recipe that was entered in the Lone Star State Food Show, sponsored by the Texas Agricultural Extension Service.

HERE'S WHAT YOU NEED:

Small amount of shortening
to grease casserole
4 medium-size sweet potatoes
½ cup unsweetened
applesauce
½ cup brown sugar

¼ cup unsweetened orange
juice
½ teaspoon nutmeg
½ teaspoon salt
1 tablespoon butter or
margarine

HERE'S WHAT YOU DO:

1. Preheat oven to 350 degrees F. Lightly grease casserole.

2. Peel sweet potatoes and cut in ½-inch slices.

3. Measure applesauce, brown sugar, orange juice, and nutmeg.

4. In the casserole, place alternate layers of sweet potatoes and applesauce. Sprinkle with sugar, juice, nutmeg, and salt.

5. Dot with butter, cover and bake for 30 to 45 minutes, or until potatoes are tender.

MAKES 4 SERVINGS

PECAN BRITTLE

An early Spanish explorer in Texas wrote: "The Indians came to the place of which we have been told to eat nuts. These are the substance of the people for several months in the year, without any other thing." Recent food studies show that pecans have important proteins and minerals and are an excellent source of quick energy.

HERE'S WHAT YOU NEED:

2 cups pecans
3 cups brown sugar
½ teaspoon salt

2 tablespoons butter or margarine

HERE'S WHAT YOU DO:

1. Grease cookie sheet or large platter.

2. Chop pecans coarsely.

3. Measure and pour sugar and salt into heavy fry pan. Place over medium heat until sugar begins to melt. Lower heat and stir until completely melted. This should be done as quickly as possible.

4. Remove fry pan from stove, and stir in pecans and add butter. Pour immediately onto cookie sheet, spreading with knife. When cool, break into pieces.

MAKES ABOUT 1½ POUNDS

UTAH

The Mormon Temple, Salt Lake City

POTATO SOUP
(St. Jacob's Soup)

When the Mormons traveled to the West by covered wagon in 1846, this easy soup was frequently cooked. The recipe has been handed down from generation to generation in the well-known Mormon family of Benjamin Morgan Roberts.

HERE'S WHAT YOU NEED:

2 large potatoes
2 large onions
8 slices bacon or ¼ pound
   salt pork

1 can (1 pound) tomatoes or
   4 fresh tomatoes
1 teaspoon salt
⅛ teaspoon pepper

HERE'S WHAT YOU DO:

1. Peel potatoes and onions and cut into small pieces.

2. Put in large saucepan and cover with water. Place over high heat. Bring to a boil and lower heat to gentle rolling boil, about 10 minutes.

3. While vegetables are cooking, cut bacon or pork into small pieces. Cook in fry pan over medium heat until golden brown, but not too crisp.

4. Remove bacon or pork with slotted spoon. Add to vegetables along with about a teaspoon of the bacon fat.

5. Add can of tomatoes and simmer for 10 minutes.

6. Season with salt and pepper.

MAKES 4 SERVINGS

ICE BOX CAKE

Utah was settled by the Mormons (members of the Church of Jesus Christ of Latter-day Saints). Through irrigation, a new idea to the West, the Mormons turned desert land into fertile soil.

This recipe is a favorite at the Mormon's Lion House Social Center, Salt Lake City. I have decreased the amount of sugar originally called for.

HERE'S WHAT YOU NEED:

1 pound vanilla wafers
½ pound (2 sticks) butter, softened
2 cups confectioners' sugar

4 eggs
1 can (1 pound) crushed pineapple
1½ cups heavy cream

HERE'S WHAT YOU DO:

1. With rolling pin, or blender, turn 1 pound of vanilla wafers into fine crumbs.

2. Place butter in large mixing bowl, and beat with mixing spoon or mixer.

3. Measure 2 cups of confectioners' sugar and slowly add to butter, continuing to beat until smooth.

4. Break eggs into separate bowl and beat lightly.

5. Gradually blend eggs into butter and sugar.

6. Open and drain can of pineapple through strainer.

7. Whip cream (see page 180). Cover and refrigerate 1 cup for topping.

(CONTINUED ON NEXT PAGE)

8. Lightly butter 8×10-inch pan. Sprinkle half of the crumbs evenly in pan. Spread butter mixture over crumbs. Spoon a layer of drained pineapple and a layer of whipped cream. Top with vanilla-wafer crumbs.

9. Cover with transparent plastic wrap and place in refrigerator overnight. Cut into 2×2½-inch squares. Top with a spoonful of whipped cream.

MAKES 16 SERVINGS

VERMONT

Fall color in Vermont, Nelson Pond, Calais

MAPLE BARS

Maple sugar is an important product in Vermont, and almost every farm has a grove of sugar maples, called an orchard or a sugar-place.

HERE'S WHAT YOU NEED:

Small amount of shortening
 to grease pan
1 cup walnuts or pecans
½ cup sugar
½ cup softened shortening
½ cup maple syrup

1 egg
⅔ cup flour
1 cup rolled oats
½ teaspoon baking powder
1 teaspoon vanilla

HERE'S WHAT YOU DO:

1. Preheat oven to 350 degrees F. Grease an 8×8-inch pan.

2. Chop nuts on cutting board with paring knife.

3. Measure and put all ingredients in large bowl. Mix thoroughly.

4. Spoon into pan and spread evenly with table knife or spatula.

5. Bake 30 to 35 minutes. Cut into squares while still warm.

MAKES 16 BARS

NEW ENGLAND BOILED DINNER

Vermont natives like typical New England cooking: chicken pie, "red flannel hash," and boiled dinners.

HERE'S WHAT YOU NEED:

1 (3 pounds) corned beef brisket	4 medium-size beets or 1 can (1 pound)
1 medium onion	4 medium-size potatoes
1 bay leaf	5 or 6 small carrots
1 teaspoon garlic powder	5 or 6 small onions
5 peppercorns	½ head cabbage

HERE'S WHAT YOU DO:

1. Wash corned beef. Place in large pot. Cover with water.

2. Peel and add 1 onion, bay leaf, garlic powder, and peppercorns.

3. When water begins to boil, lower heat, cover, and simmer about 2 hours.

4. If using fresh beets, wash and place in separate saucepan. Cover with water and boil until tender. Cool and slip skins off.

5. About 30 minutes before meat is done, peel and cut potatoes in half, scrape and wash carrots well. Peel onions. Place vegetables in pot with meat. Bring liquid to a boil and then lower to medium heat and cook about 15 minutes.

6. Cut cabbage in quarters and add along with whole beets. Cook 15 minutes.

7. Slice corned beef and serve steaming hot along with vegetables.

MAKES 4 TO 6 SERVNGS

VIRGINIA

House of Burgesses, Williamsburg

PECAN WAFFLES

Two hundred years ago, Williamsburg, Virginia, was the capital city of a colony which ran beyond the Great Lakes to the Mississippi River. Life was gay for the wealthier colonists and their food was excellent.

Today, many buildings and gardens have been restored. In the mile-long colonial city, you can eat as early Virginians did. This recipe is from Chowning's Tavern in Williamsburg.

HERE'S WHAT YOU NEED:

½ cup pecans
6 tablespoons butter
3 eggs
6 cups milk
6 cups flour
1 tablespoon baking powder
3 tablespoons sugar
1 teaspoon salt

HERE'S WHAT YOU DO:

1. Chop pecans on wooden cutting board with paring knife.

2. Melt butter in saucepan over low heat.

3. Separate egg yolks from whites (see page 179). Place each in a separate bowl. Beat yolks until thick. Measure and slowly add milk to yolks, continuing to beat. Stir in melted butter.

4. Measure flour and pour into large bowl. Measure and spoon in baking powder, sugar, and salt. Add egg and milk mixture and beat until smooth.

5. Preheat waffle iron.

(CONTINUED ON NEXT PAGE)

161

6. Beat egg whites until stiff and fold into batter along with chopped pecans.

7. Bake each waffle until it no longer steams.

Serve hot with butter and syrup.

MAKES 12 WAFFLES

SPICED PUNCH

This hot punch, also from colonial Wiliamsburg, would be pleasant to serve at a party on a cold night.

HERE'S WHAT YOU NEED:

1 quart apple cider
1 lemon
1 cinnamon stick, about 2
    inches long

6 whole cloves
½ teaspoon nutmeg

HERE'S WHAT YOU DO:

1. Pour cider into saucepan.

2. Squeeze lemon and add juice to cider.

3. Add cinnamon stick and cloves. Measure and sprinkle nutmeg over cider.

4. Place over medium heat and bring to a boil; lower heat immediately and simmer for 15 minutes. Remove cinnamon stick and cloves with slotted spoon.

Serve hot.

MAKES 8 SMALL SERVINGS

WASHINGTON

Mount Rainier and the Ohop Valley

NUT LOAF

This unusual nut loaf has a delicious flavor. While it is a long recipe, my cooking classes have found it fun.

To plan your cooking, prepare the split pea purée in advance of baking.

HERE'S WHAT YOU NEED:

1 cup Split Pea Purée (see
page 181)
1 cup nuts
Small amount of shortening
to grease pan
⅓ cup shortening, softened
1⅓ cups sugar
2 eggs

⅓ cup water
1¾ cups flour
1 teaspoon baking soda
½ teaspoon salt
¼ teaspoon baking powder
½ teaspoon cinnamon
½ teaspoon cloves
½ teaspoon nutmeg

HERE'S WHAT YOU DO:

1. Prepare Split Pea Purée.

2. Chop nuts.

3. Grease 5×9-inch loaf pan. Preheat oven to 350 degrees F.

4. Measure shortening and spoon into mixing bowl. Beat. Measure and gradually add sugar to shortening, continuing to beat.

5. Add eggs, one at a time, beating well.

6. Stir in 1 cup pea purée and ⅓ cup water.

7. Measure flour, baking soda, salt, baking powder, and spices together. Stir to blend.

(CONTINUED ON NEXT PAGE)

8. Gradually add dry ingredients to other mixture, continuing to beat. Stir in nuts.

9. Pour into loaf pan. Bake for 60 to 70 minutes.

MAKES 12 TO 18 SERVINGS

Note: Perhaps you can ask one of the adults in your house to prepare split pea soup and save 1 cup of purée for you.

FRUIT SNACKS

Washington is a leading fruit-growing state. Its products include pears, apples, cherries, peaches, apricots, and grapes.

HERE'S WHAT YOU NEED:

2 or 3 apples or pears
1 lemon (pineapple juice may
*   be substituted)*
Peanut butter or whipped
*   cream cheese*

Honey
Wheat germ or chopped nuts
Yogurt

HERE'S WHAT YOU DO:

1. Slice apples or pears in half and core with vegetable peeler. Divide halves into thin slices.

2. Cut lemon in half and squeeze juice.

3. Dip fruit slices in juice to keep them from turning dark.

4. Arrange the slices in flower-fashion on an attractive platter after doing the following:
   . . . Spread peanut butter or whipped cream cheese on several slices.
   . . . Dip some slices in honey and sprinkle with wheat germ or chopped nuts.
   . . . Dip other fruit into yogurt and sprinkle with wheat germ or chopped nuts.

MAKES 4 OR 6 SERVINGS

WEST VIRGINIA

allegheny farmland

MOLASSES COOKIES
(Cry Babies)

These West Virginia cookies have neither nuts nor fruit in them, but their molasses flavor alone makes them delicious. I imagine that the name Cry Babies came from the fact that when small children cried, they were given a cookie, don't you?

HERE'S WHAT YOU NEED:

*Small amount of shortening
    to grease baking sheet*
1 cup vegetable shortening
1 egg
1 cup sugar
1 cup dark molasses

5 cups flour
1 teaspoon ground ginger
½ teaspoon salt
1 tablespoon baking soda
¾ cup water

HERE'S WHAT YOU DO:

1. Preheat oven to 375 degrees F. Grease baking sheets.

2. Measure 1 cup shortening and spoon into large bowl. Add egg. Beat until fluffy and slowly add 1 cup of sugar.

3. Measure and add molasses. Beat again.

4. Measure flour, ginger, salt, and baking soda. Stir lightly with fork.

5. Add flour and water alternately to shortening mixture. Beat until blended.

6. Drop by teaspoonfuls on baking sheet.

7. Bake 8 to 10 minutes. Do not overcook. Cookies should have crisp crust and soft center.

8. Remove cookies and place on rack to cool.

MAKES ABOUT 70 COOKIES

HOMINY

Hominy—kernels of dried corn—is an American food, unknown in this form anywhere else in the world. It is eaten mostly in our southern states as a substitute for potatoes. When hominy is ground, it is called grits.

Luckily, you can buy canned hominy, because the cooking time for raw hominy is from 4 to 5 hours.

HERE'S WHAT YOU NEED:

1 can (1 pound) hominy
2 tablespoons butter

HERE'S WHAT YOU DO:

1. Drain liquid from can and rinse hominy in cold water.

2. Melt butter in fry pan over medium heat. Slowly add drained hominy. Stir until hot.

MAKES 4 SERVINGS

SOUTHERN CORN BREAD

My father, who was from the South, always referred to the rest of the United States as "cold bread" country. We never had a meal at home without hot bread.

Southern corn bread is flat, quite different from other corn bread.

HERE'S WHAT YOU NEED:

*Small amount of shortening
  to grease pan*
½ cup flour
1 cup white corn meal
½ teaspoon baking soda

½ teaspoon salt
1 egg
1 cup buttermilk
1 tablespoon vegetable oil

HERE'S WHAT YOU DO:

1. Preheat oven to 400 degrees F. Grease 8×8-inch pan.

2. Measure flour, corn meal, baking soda, and salt together. If you have a sifter, sift the ingredients. If not, stir lightly with a fork.

3. Beat egg.

4. Measure buttermilk and add to beaten egg.

5. Stir liquid into dry ingredients and mix until blended, no more. Measure and stir in 1 tablespoon oil.

6. Pour into pan. Bake 25 to 30 minutes, or until done (when a toothpick inserted in center comes out clean).

MAKES 6 TO 8 SERVINGS

WISCONSIN

Lush Farmland

CHEESE SNACK TRAY

Wisconsin produces almost half of the cheese eaten in this country. Why not make a cheese snack tray for yourself and friends to nibble on while playing games or watching TV.

Cheese and fruit are nutritious and taste good.

HERE'S WHAT YOU NEED:

½ package (*3 ounces*)
   American cheese
½ package (*3 ounces*)
   domestic Swiss cheese
2 *apples*

2 *pears*
Small bunch grapes (may be omitted)
12 *crisp crackers*

HERE'S WHAT YOU DO:

1. Cut cheese in strips.

2. Wash and place fruit in center of tray along with cheese strips.

3. Put crackers in a basket on tray and add small plates with table knives to cut fruit.

MAKES 4 TO 6 SERVINGS

173

SUMMER SQUASH

Squash is plentiful in Wisconsin. Whenever you can get garden-fresh vegetables, the simplest way to cook them is often the best.

HERE'S WHAT YOU NEED:

> 2 pounds yellow or green summer squash
> 3 tablespoons butter or margarine
> 1 teaspoon onion salt

HERE'S WHAT YOU DO:

1. Wash squash (do not peel) and slice thinly.

2. Melt butter in fry pan over medium heat.

3. Add squash and sprinkle with onion salt.

4. Cover and cook on low to medium heat until tender, about 5 to 10 minutes, stirring occasionally.

MAKES 4 TO 5 SERVINGS

CHERRY MILK SHAKES

Wisconsin is one of our important milk-producing states.

HERE'S WHAT YOU NEED:

2 cups (1 pint) half-and-half cream or milk
1 teaspoon cinnamon
2 cups (1 pint) cherry soda or juice drained from canned cherries

HERE'S WHAT YOU DO:

1. Measure and pour 2 cups cream or milk into pitcher.

2. Stir 1 teaspoon cinnamon into milk.

3. Add cherry soda and stir.

MAKES 4 SERVINGS

WYOMING

Cattle country

FRIED POTATOES

Potatoes are frequently served three times a day in western and mid-western states. People who do heavy work, like ranchers and sheep growers in Wyoming, need sturdy food that, as they say, "sticks to their ribs."

HERE'S WHAT YOU NEED:

4 potatoes
¼ cup shortening

HERE'S WHAT YOU DO:

1. Peel and slice potatoes about ¼ inch thick.

2. Melt shortening in heavy skillet, and fry potatoes over medium heat. Turn now and then with wide spatula.

3. Fry until tender, about 15 minutes, depending upon how thin they are sliced.

MAKES 4 SERVINGS

SHERIDAN COW BELLE BEEFBURGERS

This recipe is often served after rodeo parades in the town of Sheridan, Wyoming.

HERE'S WHAT YOU NEED:

Shortening
1½ pounds ground beef
1 medium onion
3 or 4 celery stalks
2 tablespoons brown sugar

1½ teaspoons salt
¼ cup catsup
1 tablespoon vinegar
½ teaspoon mustard

HERE'S WHAT YOU DO:

1. Melt small amount of shortening in heavy fry pan over medium heat. Fry beef until color has begun to turn.

2. Chop onion. Wash and chop enough celery to make ½ cup. Add to beef.

3. While onion and celery are cooking, measure other ingredients and add when vegetables are tender.

Serve steaming hot over buns or plain.

MAKES 4 TO 6 SERVINGS

APPENDIX

COOKING METHODS
AND BASIC RECIPES

PREPARING GREENS

Commonly cooked greens are collards, dandelion, spinach, turnip tops, and water cress.

To prepare greens for cooking, trim off roots, if any, tough portions of stalk, and imperfect leaves. Stalk may be completely discarded.

Rinse thoroughly under running water in sink. Place in large bowl and fill with water for one final rinsing. Sand clings to leaves unless rinsing is thorough.

Cook as directed.

SEPARATING EGGS

To separate egg yolk from white, crack egg in the center on the edge of a measuring cup. Make a sharp rap, then pull shell apart *slowly*. Keep yolk in one half of shell, and let white drip into cup. Pour yolk back and forth between halves of shell several times to drain egg white completely. Place egg yolk in one bowl and egg white in another.

Note: Any speck of yolk in egg white prevents it from whipping stiffly. Therefore, you should separate each egg white into a clean cup before adding to the others. A small amount of white in with the yolk is not a problem, however.

PREPARING DRY BEANS AND PEAS

Packaged beans and peas are usually sorted and washed before packing. They need only to be rinsed as follows:

Empty beans or peas into large pot. Fill slowly with water and stir. Let beans settle to bottom.

Carefully pour off water through strainer. Repeat rinsing several times.

Follow instructions in recipe for cooking.

WHIPPED CREAM

HERE'S WHAT YOU NEED:

> *1 small container (1 cup) heavy cream, chilled*
> *2 tablespoons sugar*
> *1 teaspoon vanilla*

HERE'S WHAT YOU DO:

1. If weather is warm, chill bowl and egg beater.

2. Pour cream into bowl.

3. Beat until cream begins to thicken.

4. Measure and sprinkle 1 tablespoon of sugar over cream. Beat again. Measure and add 1 tablespoon of sugar and 1 teaspoon of vanilla. Beat until stiff.

MAKES 2 CUPS WHIPPED CREAM

Note: To make 1 cup of whipped cream, use ½ cup heavy cream, 1 tablespoon sugar, and ½ teaspoon vanilla. Leftover whipped cream may be stored in a covered container in the refrigerator or freezer.

180

SPLIT PEA PURÉE

HERE'S WHAT YOU NEED:

½ cup washed split peas
1½ cups water
1 teaspoon butter or margarine

HERE'S WHAT YOU DO:

1. Measure split peas and water. Pour into heavy saucepan. Add butter or margarine.

2. Bring to boil, and reduce heat to simmer. Cover and cook for 45 minutes to an hour until soft. Stir occasionally to keep from sticking.

3. When soft, force peas through fine strainer, using wooden spoon to mash any whole ones. (Adult help may be needed when pouring.)

MAKES APPROXIMATELY 1 CUP

Note: If not used immediately, cover and store in refrigerator.

CRUMB PIE SHELL

Use for unbaked pie.

HERE'S WHAT YOU NEED:

¼ cup (½ stick) butter or margarine
¼ cup sugar
1¼ cups graham cracker crumbs

(CONTINUED ON NEXT PAGE)

HERE'S WHAT YOU DO:

1. Measure butter and spoon into medium saucepan. Melt over low heat.

2. Measure and stir in sugar. Remove from heat.

3. Measure and blend in cracker crumbs.

4. Lightly grease 8- or 9-inch pie pan. Preheat oven to 375 degrees F.

5. Spoon crumbs evenly into pie pan. Press into sides and bottom of pan with back of spoon or finger tips.

6. Bake at 375 degrees F. for 6 to 8 minutes, cool, and fill.

CEREAL PIE SHELL

Use for baked or unbaked pie.

HERE'S WHAT YOU NEED:

1¼ cups flour	½ cup corn flakes
½ teaspoon salt	⅓ cup vegetable oil
1 tablespoon sugar	2 tablespoons cold water

HERE'S WHAT YOU DO:

1. Measure flour, salt and sugar into medium-size mixing bowl.

2. Roll corn flakes into crumbs on square of wax paper with rolling pin. Add to flour.

3. Measure and add oil and water. Stir with fork until well mixed.

4. Spoon mixture evenly into 9-inch pie pan. Press into sides and bottom of pan with back of spoon or finger tips.

5. For baked pie, chill shell for 45 minutes. Fill and bake as individual recipe directs.

6. For unbaked pie, preheat oven to 450 degrees F. and bake shell for about 10 minutes, or until lightly brown. Cool and then fill.

SALAD DRESSING

HERE'S WHAT YOU NEED:

⅓ cup vinegar or lemon juice
¼ teaspoon pepper
1 teaspoon salt
1 teaspoon paprika

¼ teaspoon sugar (may be omitted)
⅔ cup vegetable oil or olive oil

HERE'S WHAT YOU DO:

1. Measure vinegar or lemon juice into jar or small bowl.

2. Measure pepper, salt, paprika, and sugar into vinegar. Stir until dissolved.

3. Measure and add oil. Stir before using. Keep covered.

MAKES 1 CUP

Note: You can place in jar with tight cover and shake thoroughly instead of stirring.

TEA

HERE'S WHAT YOU NEED:

Tea leaves or tea bags
Teapot

HERE'S WHAT YOU DO:

1. Bring fresh water to full boil in teakettle.

2. Pour small amount of hot water into teapot to warm it. Pour that water out. (You may need adult help in pouring.)

3. Place tea in teapot. The usual amount is 1 heaping teaspoon tea leaves per cup, or 1 tea bag for 2 cups.

4. Add boiling water to tea. Cover. Steep, which means to let water remain on tea leaves or bag.

5. Remove tea bag and pour, or pour through strainer to remove leaves.

INDEX

185

186

188

189

AILEEN PAUL, consumer activist and award-winning broadcaster, has taught weekly cooking classes for children in her Leonia, New Jersey, home for the past eleven years. Having tested many ideas, cooking methods, and recipes in these classes, Ms. Paul believes that children enjoy the responsibility and independence of cooking. "Children," she says, "do best when they are encouraged to make decisions that are appropriate for their age, and to follow through with those decisions and the successes or failures that result." The mother of three grown children and an active member in community affairs, Ms. Paul is the co-author (with Arthur Hawkins) of *Kids Cooking* and *Candies, Cookies, Cakes* and author of *Kids Gardening, Kids Camping, Kids Cooking Complete Meals,* and *Kids Cooking Without a Stove.*